**For my daughter Rebecca** Who lights the way

D1367744

# Contents

# Preface

*A World of Light* is a memoir of the reassembled life. In early December 1988, at the age of forty-one, I boarded a plane in Portland, Oregon, and during the flight to Washington DC, contracted a virus that targeted my brain. It was probably a common virus, according to my doctors; the most likely suspect is a human herpes virus carried on the plane's recirculated air. But my immune system was unable to stop its assault on my brain.

By the time I flew back to Oregon, three days later, I was a changed man. I knew I was very sick, but didn't perceive that the cascading symptoms were connected to a graver illness until, after six weeks of continuing deterioration, I was no longer able to work or think or remember. I couldn't run anymore, and when I tried I would get lost on the wooded trails where I'd run fifty miles a week, year after year. Used to doing a quick seventy-five pushups before breakfast, I was skipping breakfast because I could barely lift the bed covers off my body. My speech became an absurd mix of malapropisms and neologisms: *proplegate the canasta* instead of *I can't locate the can opener. I peel the night* instead of *I feel all right*, though I did not. How could an inability to remember my daughter's phone number or operate my computer or read or speak coherently be part of a lingering flu?

They were not. As brain scans finally revealed, a viral assault had eaten away parts of my brain, the resulting damage showing up as scattered punctate lesions in the cerebral cortex whose effects left me totally disabled. Connections were frayed and severed, with scar tissue scattered like frozen spots in the fiery landscape of gray matter. Computer-generated images showed what I was actually feeling inside my head: scrambled, my brain and therefore my mind pocked with holes. Neuro-physchological testing confirmed that my abstract reasoning powers, long- and short-term memory, visual learning capacity, and ability to make sense of what I see had all been severely compromised. My IQ had diminished almost twenty percent. I couldn't keep track of ongoing mental activity, couldn't calculate, spun in knotted loops of thought. I couldn't think logically, couldn't synthesize: it was impossible for me to put anything together—not a simple jigsaw puzzle, not a pair of poultry shears, seldom an idea or lucid sentence, certainly not a poem or page of prose.

More than fifteen years have passed and I remain totally disabled. Though I've relearned to read and write, and just recently began to walk again without a cane, surely the most significant advance has been to embrace fundamental changes in who I am, how I work and live, and what is important to me.

My previous book, *In the Shadow of Memory*, took eight years to write. It recounted the process by which I reassembled myself, constructing a viable sense of who I am now by examining the way brain damage changed how I think, feel, remember, maintain balance, and connect with the past. Scattered fragments of my inner experience gradually connected once I realized that it made more sense to seek harmony than mastery, and began to discover how pieces might fit, if only from moment to moment. *In the Shadow of Memory* also traced my first tentative steps back out into the world.

What I found there seemed transformed to me, and *A World of Light* recounts the process by which I have come to be at home in a shattered world. Instead of dealing with the reconstruction of a self, this book deals with the reconstruction of a life, showing what it's like to live with impaired consciousness, embracing shreds and scraps that linger in the brain-damaged mind and comprise the world as it looks to me.

I know that we all live in a shattered world. I am not alone in this.

For some, the shattering works from the outside in. Events impinge, and reality, so often crazed, explosive, or riven, can only be grasped when the impulse for order is abandoned. If the world is in pieces all around us, how can we expect to perceive it as whole?

For others, as for me, the shattering works from the inside out. I can't make things cohere, so reality often seems crazed, explosive, riven, and I must abandon the impulse for order. When perception is in tatters and time sundered, it's hopeless to seek coherence. I have learned to savor the fragments themselves, and to live in the moment. To find harmony, and the sense of being at home, smack inside the splintered spaces.

Though long-term illness often isolates and turns a person inward, I have been accompanied and brought out of myself by three extraordinary women. My wife, Beverly, so fluid and adept in her encounter with the world, shows me again and again the possibilities for transforming chaos and change into a kind of spiritual order. Throughout *A World of Light*, as I ricochet and reel inside the pandemonium of my disordered experience, she is seen to encourage, support, and often direct my efforts to find balance. Beverly is the brilliant presence that keeps me anchored in the present, and at home in the world.

Over the last half dozen years or so, as I have moved closer to integrating myself and my world, my mother has been disintegrating, losing her self and its connection with the world as she slips deeper into the chasm of Alzheimer's disease. *A World of Light* begins with my mother and never strays far from her gravitational pull. Now ninety-four, her mind eclipsed by dementia, she is with me in ways that neither of us ever imagined. We move together in counterpoint rather than in our familiar discord, given one last chance at concord by the ordinary calamity of brain damage. There is a unity in our late-life time together that defies the logic of our past. But then, neither of us is capable of much logic anymore, and our views of the past have been radically altered.

My daughter, Rebecca, now thirty-two and an accomplished writer, moves through *A World of Light* as the future moves through the past and present. Distantly most of the time, she is glimpsed from time to time in the spaces between my mother and me. Turning up at my mother's side when I could not, providing inspiration to me, taking responsibility for carrying memory forward, she gives a final clarity and hope to the story this book tells as she settles in New York, the very place where it all began, and writes books of her own.

# Acknowledgments

Chapters of *A World of Light* originally appeared in the following publications:

*The Antioch Review*: "Billy Gardner's Groundout" and "Turning Up the Gravity."

*Boulevard*: "A Pick to the Heart," "The Song of the Exhausted Well," and "A World of Light."

*Fourth Genre*: "We're Here Now" and "Thinking in Circles."

*Fugue*: "A Stable State."

*The Journal*: "The Seafood Festival Talent Show."

*Leviathan Quarterly (England)*: "The Home."

*New Hibernia Review*: "The Simple Wisdom."

*Northwest Review*: "Taking Stock."

*Prairie Schooner*: "The Home."

*River Teeth*: "Fittings."

*The Sewanee Review*: "1957."

*Southwest Review*: "The Melody Lingers On."

"The Melody Lingers On" was reprinted in *The Best American Science Writing 2003*, ed. by Oliver Sacks (Ecco, 2003) and was named a Notable Essay of 2002 by *The Best American Essays 2003*.

"Billy Gardner's Groundout" was named a Notable Essay of 2003 by *The Best American Essays 2004*.

I am grateful to The Rockefeller Foundation, which provided a residency at their Study and Conference Center in Bellagio during the time this book was nearing completion. My agent, Andrew Blauner, has been generous in his faith and friendship. Having worked with my editor, Ladette Randolph, on two books now, I know just how fortunate I am to have the benefit of her talent and judgment.

A World of Light

**part one** *We're Here Now*

# 1 The Home

Clarence is a wanderer. That's why Meg the social worker and Lucy the activities coordinator are peering through a crack between the locked doors of the Memory Impairment Unit. They need to be sure Clarence isn't poised on the other side waiting to make his escape when those doors open.

"Oh, no," Meg whispers. "He's right there."

"So is Eva," Lucy says. "Over against the wall."

They turn around to face me and Beverly. "All right, here's what we do," Meg tells us. She is a solid woman in her late thirties, authoritative but somehow gentle at the same time. Meg inspires confidence here where confidence is difficult to achieve. "When the doors open, you both walk straight in. Don't stop and don't let Clarence get hold of you. I'll take Clarence for a walk; Lucy will deal with Eva." I nod, but must look troubled because Meg adds, "Don't worry, this is normal with Alzheimer's. It's not because they're being mistreated or anything. A lot of them wander. But your mother's not a wanderer."

No, my mother is not a wanderer. In fact, at ninety she vastly prefers to perch on a chair and catch the action as it passes. Though she can ambulate with a walker, she prefers to stay put. Any aide who crosses her field of vision is asked what time it is, at which point my mother will check her wrist watch and agree. Any staff not carrying or pushing something is asked to call me on the phone so my mother can find out why I never come to visit. Any man who happens by is invited to sit beside her. If there are activities going on, she wants to be involved: she sings, she draws, she even goes on "mystery outings" where, for example, she has picked raspberries on a nearby farm, something I cannot imagine no matter how hard I try. She has been at the nursing home for a month; changes are happening to her quickly now, and not all of them seem bad. She is uncharacteristically mellow and friendly. She often smiles or hums snatches of old standards. She makes few demands or complaints, except around the issue of my visits. The problem is that she forgets them as soon as Beverly and I leave, and is convinced we never come to see her though we are there at least weekly. We have bought a wall calendar for her on which to note our visits, but know she will not remember to look at it.

Not a wanderer, not incontinent, astonishingly healthy for someone who smoked Chesterfields for sixty years and was always overweight and never exercised, my mother is thriving now that we have moved her from New York to Oregon. But, though she has not been diagnosed with Alzheimer's disease, her memory impairment is severe and progressing steadily. After a month of transition in the nursing home's Intermediate Care Unit, she has been recommended for the Memory Impairment Unit where she can receive more appropriate, concentrated support. This is also where Clarence and Eva live, and where we are all going for a tour if we can charge in without letting the others escape.

Before she turns back to open the door, I ask Meg if everyone in the unit spends the whole day trying to get out. I wonder if this is the right move for my mother.

"Oh no, just Clarence and sometimes Eva. If she sees him waiting by the door, she follows. The rest are like your mother, and we take them out for all the usual activities." She places a hand on my arm for a moment. "Really, don't worry. If you don't feel good about this, we won't move your mother at all."

The door is opened, and Clarence is led out. Head down, arms raised to wedge aside any further obstacles, he nods as he rumbles like a fullback toward the lobby. As the doors close, Lucy and I elude a stunned Eva. But Beverly—who is a hospice social worker and deeply empathetic toward the elderly—stops in front of her, smiling. Eva is tense and wants to go after Clarence, but relaxes as Beverly speaks. She smiles back, nods. Then her eyes flick toward the door and she tries an end-run to Beverly's right. Moving with Eva, never restraining her, keeping her verbally engaged, Beverly gets her to settle down.

An obviously relieved Lucy leans back against the wall and begins to ask me about my mother's history. She says my mother is charming, cooperative, and talented, a joy to work with. We chat about my mother's easy adjustment; then out of the corner of my eye I see Jessica Tandy edging her way toward us.

"Hello, Millie," Lucy says when Jessica Tandy reaches us. "Millie, this is Floyd. His mother will be moving onto the unit soon."

Jessica Tandy—Millie's resemblance to the late actress is too striking to ignore—keeps moving closer to Lucy, even though she's already in contact with her. It seems at first as though she's trying to crawl inside Lucy's skin, which I imagine as another form of escape. But then I see she has gripped Lucy's upper arm and is squeezing it, crowding the younger woman against the wall. Her knuckles and Lucy's biceps whiten.

"I know what you're up to," Jessica Tandy hisses. "Don't think you can fool me."

"That's all right, Millie."

"You shameless hussy!"

Now Lucy is trying to disentangle herself and I can see that Jessica Tandy is beginning to turn toward me. I'm next, and don't want to imagine what Ms. Tandy has in store for me, so I wave to Lucy and head for the doors, where Beverly waits.

Outside again, in the lobby, I see that Meg has led Clarence to a plush easy chair and is bringing my mother over to meet him. We join them just in time for the introductions.

"Clarence," Meg says, "I'd like you to meet Lillian. She'll be moving onto the unit."

Clarence lifts his hand and places it over his eyes, turning his head away. My mother, whose memory may be shattered but whose flirting instincts remain intact, moves closer to him.

"Hello, Clarence," she says, her voice suddenly deepening.

He turns his head further away, eyes totally hidden.

"Say hello," she coos. "Come on, Clarence."

He sinks further into his chair.

"All right, then. We can meet later." She looks in my direction and smiles. "Floyd! What are you doing here?"

They might as well hang a sign in front of The Home saying "Welcome All!" As life span increases, more and more elderly people inhabit bodies that have outlived their minds. This is surely why *Newsweek*, in a 1998 cover story, discovered that memory was the main health worry of baby boomers. The chairman of Harvard's Psychology Department, Daniel L. Schacter, says in his book *Searching for Memory* that "decades of research leave little doubt that aging can impair memory." He notes that "overall brain mass steadily shrinks as we enter our sixties and seventies, at roughly 5 percent to 10 percent per decade." Blood and oxygen flow to the brain diminishes; the frontal lobes shrink; the hippocampus, cornerstone in forming explicit memories and developing our sense of self, atrophies; the basal forebrain, implicated in most amnesias, loses neurons and lessens the production of essential memory chemicals. All this happens in "healthy" aging brains. The situation is even more dire in the brains of people with Alzheimer's disease.

So the longer we live, the more certainly we should begin queuing up for space in The Home. And while we inch closer to the doors, we can imagine what living with a damaged system of memory will be like. In daily life, especially in busy daily lives, memory's normal unreliability offers us glimpses of what my mother or Clarence or Eva are experiencing: a frustrated scramble through your house in search of the lost appointment book that you're carrying in your hand; the smiling man striding across a room toward you with his hand outstretched and saying how good it is to see you again, though you have

no idea who he is; the name of that woman you played rac-
quetball with last month, it's on the tip of your tongue, the
one you'd like to call because you have an extra ticket to see
*Carmen*; that sailing trip you took with your older brother on
Lake Michigan, which he says never happened. These are each
different forms of forgetting, of memory's lapses. Most of the
time, they are normal occurrences, not signs of illness but signs
that memory is doing what it is designed to do, ridding itself of
inessential matter, uncluttering. But as age-related dementia
sets in, such forgetting intensifies and worsens, eradicating
even the most essential matter, until nothing is left.

I find myself coming through the doors of The Home now
with a triple sense of distress. Not only is my mother there and
her condition worsening, not only are we all headed there, but
I have sustained the kind of damage that might accelerate my
movement up the queue. Every time I visit my mother, I also
feel myself being whisked back to 1988, to Washington DC. I
become aware of a creepiness inside the cranium, as though
actually experiencing, in real time and as a physical sensation,
the invasion of those lesions speckling my frontal lobes, throwing neurochemicals out of balance, fraying cerebral nerve
endings, bringing me closer and closer to The Home. Just
this week, I have twice forgotten the name of my newly published book, tried to plug the coffee maker into the vent on
the microwave, left my wallet in the car while bringing the
tire gauge inside and placing it on the shelf where my wallet
goes, phoned my doctor when I meant to phone my Internet
service provider, and said I walk with a horn when I meant
to say I walk with a cane. If tested by The Home's staff on a
bad day, I'm afraid I might qualify for a room—my mother's
dream come true.

We are accompanying my mother down the hall. A plastic tag
printed with her name has been wound around her walker's
cross bar and she stops to point this out to us.
"Look! It says my name."
"Yes. That's because this is your walker."

"This is my walker?"

I nod and my mother begins moving again. After three steps, she looks down and stops. "Look! This thing has my name on it."

Beverly answers, "That's right, Mother. Lillian Rosen."

"Lillian Rosen? That's my name?"

We take a few more steps and stop. She points toward the plastic tags. "Look here! What does this say?"

"It says your name: Lillian Rosen," I tell her. When she looks up again, eyes turning toward the solarium that is our destination at the hallway's end, I flip the tag over so it dangles downward and won't distract her.

We take three more steps and she stops, looks down, and frowns. "Where is that tag? My name is gone!" She is getting agitated, a mood whose resonances I recognize deep in my bones and haven't felt emanating from her since she has moved here. "Someone must have taken my walker."

I touch her shoulder, sorry for having messed things up, and flip the tag back upright. "No, it was just hidden. Here we go, this is your walker after all."

"This is my walker?"

We are all nodding now, catching our breath. I point toward the solarium, but my mother looks back down to check things out.

"See?" I ask. "Lillian Rosen's walker."

"I should give it back to her," my mother says. "Because I have one of my own. It has my name on it."

There is nothing to be done about my mother's wrecked short-term memory system. She will only get worse, each instant vanishing into the next without continuity. But there is a remote hope that her long-term memory can still be stimulated.

We have brought a series of framed photographs and placed them around my mother's half of the room. The nurses and residential care manager have told us that photos are very important. There is one of me and Beverly, a little out-of-date now according to the lack of grizzle in my beard and the length of Beverly's blond hair. There is a nice one of my daughter Becka and her then-husband Gualtiero. In the last two years, my mother saw them several times, when she still lived in New York, and they traveled up from Pittsburgh to visit. She was dazzled by Gualtiero's good looks and warmth, almost as much as by his Italian name and accent. Before her symptoms began their final worsening, she loved telling him that she once lived for a year in Rome, so she was practically an Italian native. With a flutter of her eyes, she would say a few words to Gualtiero in Italian. Why, if Becka wasn't careful, my mother would say, she just might lose her husband to her own grandmother. We've given Becka's photo pride-of-place on the bedside table. Nearby is a large photo of my mother's brother Al, who died about fifteen years ago. They were eighteen months apart in age and he was someone, perhaps the only person I could remember, that my mother adored without restraint or criticism. There is also a photo of her second husband, Julius Rosen, a man to whom she was married for a quarter century after my father's death.

Visits commence with an examination of these images. A few months ago, my mother was having trouble recalling the faces, so Becka taped the relevant information on the back of each: "Beverly and Floyd—Lillian's son and daughter-in-law;" "Becka and Gualtiero—Lillian's granddaughter and grandson-in-law." But now my mother either forgets that the labels are there, or removes and places them on different pictures. I think that when her brother becomes her second husband and her granddaughter becomes her daughter-in-law, it perfectly reflects the state in her mind. I can never decide whether the presence of these pictures helps or haunts my mother.

"Who is this?" she says, holding the one of me and Beverly. She looks from the picture to my face and then to Beverly's, looks back down, back up, and her eyes widen. "This is you!"

"That's right. Me and Beverly."

"Who?"

"Beverly," I say, and nod toward the closet where Beverly is examining the condition of my mother's clothes.

My mother's voice lowers toward a whisper. "She's a beautiful girl. You ought to marry her."

She replaces the picture and picks up the one of Becka and Gualtiero. "Do I know these people?"

"That's your granddaughter," I tell her. "Becka."

"I have a granddaughter?" When I nod she shakes her head vigorously and says, "Can't be."

"Why not?"

"I'm not old enough." She looks at me to see what I will say to that.

I realize she is not sure how old she is, or if she's even "old" at all. I also begin to sense that she's not certain who I am, or how we might be connected. In the last month, she has mistaken me for her husband, her grandson, her last boyfriend, and her doctor, though initially—upon first seeing my face or hearing my voice—she knows me to be Floyd and her son. As visits progress, though, or as she tires, facts blur. She is puzzled now, looking at the picture, then at me, then at the skin of her hand that holds the picture. The hand captures her attention. She puts the picture down and runs a finger over the wrinkled surface of her other hand. "How old *am* I?" she finally asks.

"You're ninety."

"Ninety? I certainly am not."

"It's true, Mother; you'll be ninety-one in October."

"October 14!" she announces, smiling. "And don't you forget my birthday, either. I want chocolate." But her mood stays foggy; she reaches for the picture and notices her hand again, then looks up at me, her expression unstuck, bewildered. "I was born in 1910, wasn't I?"

"Yes, and it's 2001."

She begins some kind of count, folding fingers in turn, then shakes her head. "How old am I?"

"Ninety."

She sighs. "Don't say that."

Turning the photo back over, she asks again who these people are.

"That's Becka and Gualtiero."

"What kind of name is that? Quateero?"

"It's Italian." She does not respond. "You lived in Italy for a year, Mother. Remember?"

She shakes her head. "Why would I do a thing like that?"

I reach for the photo of her brother, ready to change the subject as she wishes, alarmed by how far and how fast she has deteriorated. This was always her favorite photo; it was taken at a ski resort in Switzerland, probably sometime in the late 1970s. Al was nearing seventy but looks much younger despite his graying hair.

"Who is that boy?" she asks.

"This is your brother."

"Oh, Albie." She closes her eyes, shakes her head. "It's so sad. That was taken when he was in high school. Yes, yes. He died when he was a baby, you know. I never got over it."

At this point in her life, with long-term memory shredded and short-term memory limited to about ten seconds, my mother seems to be living entirely in the moment. I wonder if this is a horrible, labyrinthine trap for her or a release, a form of salvation, even grace. Struggling to spend time with her, driven batty by the aimless and repetitive chatter, I tell myself to abandon expectations or hope for a "relationship," to just be in the moment with her. But I find myself wanting to know if she is as peaceful and accepting as she often seems.

She can ask certain questions that seem to obsess her—who is married to whom, what to do next, what time it is, how old she is—and sometimes respond to an answer, but can get no further in conversation than that initial exchange. She appears content to sit near The Home's front desk and watch the action, though she would never have tolerated such passive entertainment before, nor accepted a role on the margins. Seeing her sitting there when we arrive unannounced, before she has spotted us, I see her expression and cannot recognize it. She looks bemused, sweetly present, attentive. Or is the expression one of absence rather than presence? My mother was always a huge presence, filling up the space around her with her extravagant clothing and gestures, voice raised in a variety of accents and tones delivering critical commentary or demanding attention, interrupting conversations. *Just a minute! Excuse me! Just a minute!* Now I cannot always find her when I enter a room she's in. From across the room, it comes to me with the force of revelation: the problem is mine; I must learn to live in the moment with her now, to let go of the past myself.

She does not seem to think about the past or even have access to it, never referring to it spontaneously, never finding answers to probing questions. My father and brother, both dead, are gone from her mind, even when she is given cues. She doesn't remember that she ever lived in New York or that she recently relocated. What matters, if her remarks are a reliable guide, is the eternal Now, and the tense she uses is the present.

"Is it time to eat yet?" she asks as soon as the greetings are done.

"No, Mother, it's only 2:30." I don't tell her that we must leave in an hour.

She checks her watch and says, "It's 2:30." Then she lifts her hand and listens to make sure the watch is still running. "I'm so glad you've come for dinner."

We suggest a walk down the hall to her room. Between stops to discuss the name tag on her walker, to reconsider whether it's time to eat or to examine the photographs beside each door that help residents identify their own rooms, the twenty-yard trip takes ten minutes.

"How are you feeling, Mother?" Beverly asks.

My mother stops walking, looks up at Beverly, and says, "I don't know."

"Well, you look great."

She smiles at that, raises a hand to her cheek—which is remarkably smooth—and says, "But where are the men?" Then she rotates her head from where Beverly has been standing to where I am standing and says, "Floyd! What are you doing here?"

Everyone at The Home who deals with my mother says she is happy. She is easy to work with, content as long as someone tells her exactly what to do at any given moment, where to sit, what item of clothing to put on next, what bit of food to eat next, what to do if she has to go to the bathroom. With those issues resolved—though the answer is forgotten almost immediately—she is cooperative and cheerful. I see her acting in ways I have never seen before: responding politely to questions from strangers, especially from staff at The Home, from people she would have considered lower class; smiling at fellow residents even if they are female, even if they speak with strange accents; trying new things like that trip to a raspberry farm. She wears leisure clothing, even sweat pants; I've never seen my mother in pants before.

Her relative calm, her equanimity, are almost more shocking to me than her past flamboyance and casual disdain had been. But, I wonder, is she really happy? Is this what happiness looks like for someone like my mother? Perhaps, stripped of her past, it is true that she has been liberated by living solely in the moment.

I must admit, her situation at The Home exceeds what I have hoped for. That my mother would be like this instead of consumed by rage, that she would find peace and happiness near the end, that I would be able to help her in some way and be useful to her. Yet I am uneasy. Wary. It is ridiculous, I know it is, but I still find it difficult to trust my mother in the moment, even though that's all we have now. She is, it appears, released; she is at peace, as the experts here have been telling me. The terms are clear enough: I need to share the moment with her and let the rest go.

What we have finally available is the form of a relationship I've yearned for, but without the substance. I will have to accept that this is so, the best we can do together, and stop watching like a raptor for that flicker in my mother's eyes that says *I know. I remember.*

When she sees me for the first time each visit, we embrace and go over the same script. It begins with a kiss on the cheek.

"Oh, Floyd!" she gasps. "I'm so glad you're here."

"It's good to see you."

"And Beverly!" They hug and my mother says, "Oh, dear, you're so beautiful. You two should get married."

After we assure her that we are married, my mother's expression changes, and she says, "I wondered if you'd ever come again. It's been so long."

"No, Mother, it hasn't. We were here five days ago."

"You were?"

"We come every week."

My mother then shakes her head slowly, lifts her right hand to her brow, and frowns. Then she perks up again, looks at Beverly, looks at me, smiles, and says, "Floyd! Beverly! It's so good to see you at last. This is the happiest day of my life."

# 2  We're Here Now

I spent my adult life getting as far away as possible from my mother. For nearly forty years I moved steadily west from her home on Long Island's south shore, living in Pennsylvania, Illinois, Washington, and, finally, Oregon. My brother followed the same pattern. He went to New Jersey, then California, where he lived for nearly a quarter century till his death at fifty-seven. He would not even answer his phone, assigning that responsibility to his wife, since the caller might be our mother.

She was a flamboyantly disappointed, tyrannical, violent woman. Would-be aristocrat, thwarted star of stage and screen, silenced chanteuse, potential rival of Mary Cassatt, my mother married a butcher and believed herself under sentence in their tiny Brooklyn apartment. Her illusions of noble privilege and patrician style were desecrated; nothing was as it should have been. Not even when we moved to Long Island in 1957, where the sandy beach and briny air only provoked her to rage. For years I thought mothers normally bit deep gouges into their own wrists when children spilled a glass of milk, then grabbed them by an ear, marched them into the bedroom, made them empty their toy chests, stuffed them inside and locked the lid for two hours. I assumed "flu" was the medical term for a black eye, and the real reason other kids were absent from school too. I imagined all boys and girls listened while their mothers dialed the phone, asked to talk to the director of the county hospital's "insane unit," and asked if there was a room available for a little boy who disobeyed his mother. The only one available was next to The Mad Bomber? *That'll be fine. Tomorrow, if he doesn't start behaving.*

Having come to think of my childhood as The Big Bang, I saw my adulthood as a gradual slowing down of the family dispersal that childhood initiated. In time I settled into distant orbit; my mother remained on Long Island, her heat, her pull, still felt. We spoke by long distance. Occasionally Beverly and I flew back for brief visits, but it never felt safe or even possible for me to linger. Then last year, when it was clear my mother could no longer live on her own, Beverly and I brought her to Oregon. She lives an hour away from us. We are realigned.

I know this is not a unique situation, but our particulars have a singular strangeness. I am fifty-five now, the signs and symptoms of brain damage still as evident as they were when I first got sick. My mother is ninety-one and more firmly in the grip of her dementia. It is as though chance and fate have reasserted our inherent connectedness, dealing our brains complementary blows.

Neither of us is as we were anymore. Our memories have, to varying degrees, been shattered. As a result, the past we shared looks very different now: hers has vanished; mine is in random tatters with the most vivid, most intense memories enduring whole, probably because such memories are stored in a separate part of the brain, one that escaped the primary damage. Our brains have both undergone vast organic alter-ation and our minds no longer work as they did. So maybe, out of this weird wreckage, we can find something in the time we have left together that is better than what we found in the past.

This turn of events offers an opportunity for us to draw together at last. Offers? It insists. Because not only has our remembered past been radically rearranged, but so has our future. A month ago she was diagnosed with breast cancer.

When Beverly and I arrive at the nursing home, my mother is playing bingo. She sits at a long table among two dozen residents, hunched over her card, face inches from its surface, shaking her head. Adamantly. Macular degeneration may have ravaged her vision and dementia destroyed her memory, but she still sees well enough and focuses closely enough to know her card is not filling up the way it should.

"Stupid caller," she mutters. "Can't even announce the numbers properly." She looks around, then places a marker over B-32, though the number called was B-23. "There!"

I pull a chair next to her. She no longer smells of cigarette smoke and heavy makeup. Her eyelashes are no longer darkened shanks. She is annoyed at the way this game is developing, at how difficult it is to see and keep track of her card. She hates when other residents win the game's twenty-five-cent prize. She grumbles at the aide who strolls between tables offering help and at the resident in a wheelchair to her right who keeps repeating the caller's announcements. I know she does not remember we were coming, and within moments of our departure will forget we were there. She will then demand that a nurse phone me at home, well before I have gotten there, to find out when we are finally coming to visit. If we are not available to take her call, she will be annoyed all over again.

But she will be delighted when I make my presence known. Since it is the one moment of her delight that I can count on during a visit, I savor the anticipation. This is a new phenomenon in my life. There will be an instant when she is not sure who I am, then another when she is not sure I am real. But I will say, *Hello, Mother* and then she will gasp: *Oh!* Her eyes will widen. She will touch my arm, just to be sure, then announce, *It's you! Oh, this is the happiest day of my life.*

Before arriving at this nursing home last year, my mother was never a bingo player. Bingo, she would have said, was a game for the hoi polloi. For people who drove their own cars, or wore uninsured jewels and domestic rather than imported fashions. People who ate stews. After all, did the nobility play such nonsense? Besides, bingo had a nasty mixture of narrowed fate—the card you were handed—and too much left to chance. It was simply a lottery and lotteries were, she felt, for the lower classes. In Brooklyn, when my father was alive, they hosted card parties at which she consented to play canasta with the women while he played poker with the men. Mahjong was possible, and in later life, with her second husband, Scrabble. Games of great skill, she felt. But bingo? About as likely as competition tiddlywinks.

As her dementia accelerated, my mother found herself compromising. She had increasing trouble managing her customary two-hour costuming routine in the morning and sustaining balance in her tight high-heeled shoes. Her last boyfriend, in the retirement hotel back in New York, was an eighty-five-year-old former mechanic who knew nothing of the fine arts and wore comfortable polyester pants. A man who winked, who took walks; a man who played bingo. As cognitively impaired as she was, he turned out to be fine, undemanding company and they spent most of their time sitting in the lobby where other residents could see them and, my mother hoped, be jealous. She never called him by his first name, Irv, conveying her disdain by referring to him only as Dorfman. But now she herself not only plays bingo, she dresses in a T-shirt and cardigan, sweat pants and sandals. Her hair is its natural gray. She adorns herself with two beaded necklaces she made in the arts and crafts room. And though she is ticked off about the way this game is going, my mother is more civil and temperate than I ever remember her being.

"N-17" the caller says.

My mother studies her card and finds the correct square. She snatches another marker and is ready when B-4 is called.

"Before what?" she mutters. Now, with her card beginning to look a bit better, she smiles.

"I think you're going to win," I tell her.

She waves my words away, still smiling. She gets two more squares.

"You're on a roll, Mother."

At that, she turns toward me and says, "Mother?" She leans closer, peering. "Who's that?"

"Hello, Mother."

"Floyd!" she gasps, touching my arm. "It's you!" She spreads her fingers over her chest and rolls her eyes. "Oh, this is the happiest day of my life."

We hug. Beverly moves into my mother's visual range and triggers another gasp. "Oh! And, oh, and it's," my mother says.

"Beverly," my wife says, joining the embrace. "How are you today?"

"Beverly!" My mother makes a sound that is partway between a laugh and a sob. Then she lets us go and says, "Let me look at you."

We are all smiling. This is a scene that would have been impossible to envision at any other time in my life. I savor it: my mother this openly happy, nothing complicating the moment, everyone embracing, love all around. What next, Lassie barking as she nuzzles my mother's hand?

"Oh!" my mother says again. "She's so beautiful, Floyd. You two should get married already."

"We are married," I tell her. "Nine years next week."

"Nine years?" The expression on her face begins to change. We can watch the happiness melting away. She frowns and says, "When will you come again?"

"We just got here."

"I know, but when will you come again? Do I have to wait another nine years?"

My mother loves excursions now. It doesn't matter where we go or what we do; she's pleased just to be in motion. This is apparently true inside the nursing home as well, where we are told that my mother never sits in her room or lies down for a nap. She cannot entertain herself, though she is happy to entertain an audience. She cannot bear to be still or alone. *What do I do now?* she continually asks the staff. They tell her, and off she goes, smiling.

After checking her room to see if there is anything she needs, Beverly and I lead my mother out to the car. She takes a few steps within the scaffolding of her walker, then stops to speak.

"You're taking me out?"

"For coffee and cookies."

"Oh!" She takes a few more steps and stops. "This is the happiest day of my life!"

After another small progression toward the driveway, she stops to say, "Where are we going?"

"To Starbucks for coffee and cookies."

"Oh! You're taking me out?" I nod. She takes a few steps and stops. "You know, I would like to go out for coffee and cookies. Can we do that?"

"Good idea."

When we reach the street, she stops and looks up. "It rains every time you come here."

Because this is just the kind of thing my mother would have said in her prime, and because her husky voice sounds like it always did, I am suddenly angry. I needed to drive an hour into Portland for this? Hey, it always rains in Portland. It's not my fault!

She moves again, pushing the walker ahead, smiling a little. She stops and blinks when rain hits her face, then says, "You're here." She approaches the car and says, "I can't believe my eyes." I take the walker, and my mother, leaning against Beverly to negotiate her way into the front seat, says, "She's beautiful." Beverly helps her settle, buckles her in. "You two should get married already." I walk around the car, seeing through the windshield that my mother is still talking, though Beverly and I cannot hear her now. As we settle into the car, my mother says, "Day of my life." I turn on the windshield wipers. "It rains every time you come here."

All I can do is laugh. There is, of course, no point in being angry. I must find a way to avoid this instinctive response to her voice and tone, because she means nothing by it. The words have little real significance, and she no longer has the vital capacity to intend cruelty, to manipulate. At worst, her response and its tone are simply vestigial.

There are, naturally, two Starbucks coffee shops within a mile of the nursing home. The one to the west requires a tricky left turn across three lanes of oncoming traffic; the one to the east requires only a simple right turn.

"When will you come see me again?"

"We just got here!"

"I'm so glad to see you."

"It's good to see you, too."

"So when will you come to see me again?"

I decide to turn right. Keep things simple; minimize the risks.

"In three or four weeks," I say, though I don't want to talk about the diminishing frequency of our visits.

"Three or four weeks? That's wonderful!"

"We come every three or four weeks."

Her voice deepens and darkens. "Every three or four weeks?" She shakes her head. "No good. If I had a mother, I would see her every day."

She has a point. An hour's drive seems long to me because I dread our time together, and how exhausted I feel for the next few days. We used to visit every week, when she first got to Oregon. Then every two weeks. Now every three or four weeks. I believe I am balancing concern for myself with concern for my mother, but I know she would not see it that way.

Once we are at Starbucks sipping drinks and nibbling cookies at a table, I notice how tense I have been. My leg and shoulder muscles ache, as does my head. I have been perched on the edge of the seat, focused intently on everything going on, responding to everything my mother says, cleaning up crumbs, reminding her to eat her cookies, drink her coffee. *This is ridiculous*, I tell myself, and realize I have just used my mother's voice to make that observation.

When I am home, even when I am heading to Portland for these visits, I understand they do not have to be ordeals. Her volatile personality has lost much of its edge; she is calmer and more capable of those instants of simple happiness. If the past tinges our time together now, it is because of me, and what I import into that time. I am free to leave the past behind and allow each encounter with my mother to be as fresh for me as it seems to be for her. A new start for us, each moment arriving without historical baggage. A chance to have an uncomplicated interlude together, for as long as she may have left. It might lack the content of a genuine mother-son intimacy, but it can resemble that connection in ways that might be moving, perhaps healing. I know and believe all that.

Then I hear her voice, or a gesture triggers memories, or I catch a resonance in what she says (*it rains every time you come here*) that may not be there, and opportunity starts its transformation into ordeal. Usually, Beverly's smile will be enough to bring me out of it. I take a long breath, my mother moves on to the next stop along her narrow loop of topics, and I see things for what they are. But I know I am making these visits more difficult than they need to be. I must remember what it is possible to expect from my mother. Then I must recognize it for what it is, and accept that her happiness in seeing us is genuine, her anxiety about the frequency of our visits is understandable, and her momentary delight is the only delight on offer.

"Do you like your cookie, Mother?"

"What kind is it?"

"Chocolate chip."

She reaches for a piece, holds it up, and says, "This is the best cookie I've ever tasted." She puts the piece down and picks up another. "Next time, maybe I could have chocolate chip instead."

We have left Starbucks and entered a Fred Meyer One Stop Shopping store. My mother loves these places, reacting to the lights and merchandise with childlike glee. But today she is having trouble getting beyond the questions in her mind. She hardly notices where we are.

"When will you come see me again?"

"Soon, Mother. We come every few weeks."

"I'm so glad." She takes a few steps and stops. "How many years is it since you visited me last?"

"We're here now." I mean, of course, that we are visiting at this moment, so why not enjoy it now. But I also gesture toward a rack of lipsticks. Beverly, who moved ahead of us, selected an assortment to show my mother.

"Where?" my mother says. The ambiguity of my statement has made her even more confused than usual. "Where are we?"

"In the store, buying you lipstick."

"And look!" she says. "Your girlfriend's here. Isn't that a surprise. When are you two going to get married?"

"We are married, Mother."

"You are? How long?

"Nine years."

"Nine years. But you'll come again in a few weeks?"

"Absolutely." I point to the lipsticks in Beverly's hand and say, "We'll even buy you more lipstick."

She nods, looks down, and says, "But why do you have that stick in your hand?"

"It's a cane, Mother. I've been using a cane for fourteen years now."

"You have? Why?"

Even before her dementia worsened, my mother could not or would not remember my illness. It embarrassed her; it made no sense. *A virus? You caught a virus on a plane trip and it damaged your brain? Are you sure your doctor knows what he's doing?* No matter how many times I told her that I was disabled, that I could not work, that I was sick, she never accepted my illness. *You have memory problems? So what, I have them too. You're just getting a little older. Besides, nobody I know has brain damage.* Brain damage, like bingo, was not an acceptable turn of events.

"I'm sick," I answer. "I need the cane to keep my balance."

"You're sick?" She looks intently at my face. For an instant, I wonder if she is going to check my brow for fever. "What's wrong with you?"

I put my hand around her shoulder and give her a hug. "I caught a virus that targeted my brain." She's still looking at me, trying to see, trying to comprehend something. I realize that one aspect of my anxiety over our visits is connected with fear. I can see in my mother's ravaged mind one possible future for my own. I'm her son, with half my genes inherited from this woman. I can only hope I have her longevity, and that the virus responsible for my brain damage has not hastened me along her path toward senility.

I also realize that I must have deeper compassion for her. This means I must think about her, and allow for tenderness, when five decades have accustomed me to blocking all thoughts of her. I must also, and finally, accept her as she is, not as she was and not as I wish her to be. Which is, after all, what I always wanted her to do for me.

I smile at her, the explanation of my condition now finished. My mother blinks and turns toward Beverly.

"It's you!" She beams. "Oh, dear, imagine finding you here." She accepts the lipstick from Beverly and says, "I wonder where Floyd is? Do you know what he looks like?"

Although my mother no longer has access to her long-term memories and cannot form new ones, she does not seem to be lost in time. Instead, I imagine she is frozen in the Now. When I mention that she lived in New York for ninety years, she denies it. No, she never sang on WBNX as "The Melody Girl of the Air." No, she never was married to a butcher, did not spend years making greeting cards from castoff buttons, or play Agnes Gooch in a community theater version of *Auntie Mame*. Her parents, two husbands and brother; her older son who died and the beloved cousins from New Haven; New Haven itself, which she considered the most elite city in the East because her cousins lived there: all gone from her mind. Sometimes Beverly and I will find her sitting alone in the solarium, eyes closed. After the greeting, she cannot remember where she was when we arrived. *How did we get here? I like this room.* She says she was not thinking of anything, and I have come to believe her. She was not sitting there plotting, churning over imagined wrongs. She is convinced, simultaneously, that we have not visited her in years and that we are still engaged in our previous visit. Time has scant meaning for her, though she worries about its passage between visits.

There is, in the worst sense, nothing for her to keep track of beyond the immediate moment. Nothing else ever seems to have happened or be about to happen. Yet, because each moment has a host of potential associations—*this is my son; this is his beautiful girlfriend what's-her-name, who he should marry; I am somewhere*—she can keep track of nothing.

Though this seems like torture, my mother still usually remains equable now, according to reports we get from the nursing home staff. The thing that seems to agitate her the most is me. My presence suggests a past and a future she cannot grasp, cannot bring into focus. I think her efforts to figure out when we last visited, and when we will visit again, are her way of making sense of an elusive feeling of continuity that I trigger for her. Or, perhaps, of horrible discontinuity. She misses me most when I am actually there, because that is the time when she remembers that I was not.

In the early stages of my own illness, I had similar difficulties. Short-term memory was unreliable and long-term memory erratic. Days whizzed by, though time seemed to have stopped. But gradually time took shape again for me. I patched together a coherent sense of my past, working around the gaps and ragged edges, and grasped possibilities for my future. I also came away with a greater appreciation for the present moment. My mother is not graced with this good fortune. Time only spirals more wildly for her. I have had glimpses of that myself and feel terrified for her.

After a few months at the nursing home, we were told, the passage of time was becoming unmanageable for my mother and consequently for the staff working with her. When there were no organized activities, she had begun lashing out at the nurses, aides, and other guests, calmness gone, the old behaviors reasserting themselves. We had a meeting with the staff; they were considering the need for a psychiatric consultation and, perhaps, medication to help control her anxiety and explosive anger. But first, they thought, we should all pay a visit to the home's day-care center. Maybe a few days a week in day care, every moment filled with something for my mother to do, would be worth the investment for everyone concerned. And keep her off psychotropic drugs. Yes, they said, why not have a look at the facility; go see Arnie.

We found my mother in her room, standing at the bathroom mirror, smiling. Such bathroom sessions, we had been told during the meeting, were among the few things my mother does by herself. She sometimes remains in front of the mirror for fifteen minutes. It is, for her, an Activity.

"Floyd! It's you!" She turned back to the mirror and adjusted a pair of beaded necklaces that she had made the week before. Then she turned back and said, "Floyd! It's you! Oh, this is the happiest day of my life."

We led her into the hall. She stopped her walker in the doorway of her room, pointed to her photograph beside the door, and said, "This is my room." Then she took a few steps, stopped, and said, "You never come to visit me."

The walk from the Memory Impairment Unit to the day-care center took about fifteen minutes. Yes, Beverly and I are married. Nine years now. Yes, she is beautiful. We were here a couple of weeks ago, and we will return soon.

"Welcome!" Arnie said as soon as we entered the day-care center. He beamed. Small, tanned, white-haired, and full of warmth, Arnie radiated hospitality. He was so glad to meet my mother, had heard so much about her. He patted me on the back, shook Beverly's hand, smiled at my mother.

"I hear you're quite a singer," he told her.

"I am?" my mother said.

"We sing every day here." His hand swept outwards, directing our attention across the room. "We sing, we tell stories, we share, we have programs, we play games. You'll love it."

At the far end, by the windows with their view of young Douglas fir, a net sagged in the afternoon light. Four wheelchairs were ranged on either side of the net, their occupants batting a balloon back and forth. Senior volleyball. Everyone seemed engaged in the game.

Arnie took both of my mother's hands in his. "I also hear you're a very fine artist. Would you enjoy painting here?"

My mother smiled. She actually batted her eyes at Arnie. "Of course, dear. If you're here."

I remembered taking my daughter to a day-care program just like this, run by Annie instead of Arnie. I never would have imagined my mother playing volleyball, but it seemed possible that she would enjoy being there, and that the break for the staff on the Memory Impairment Unit would make it easier for them to work with her on the off-days.

As we headed back toward her room, I told my mother that she would be going to the day-care program three times a week.

"Three times a week?"

"Tuesday, Wednesday, and Thursday."

"Oh, Floyd!" She stopped and looked at me. "You'll visit me three times a week? That's wonderful."

My mother has three significant lumps in her left breast and one massive lump in her right. Late-life breast cancer works its sabotage slowly, and no one involved in my mother's care believes it makes sense to put her through intrusive testing, a double mastectomy, and chemotherapy. She forgets the doctor's visits as soon as he leaves her room, is symptom-free, and remains unaware of her illness. The doctor said this cancer may not even be what ends her life, given its languid progression in a woman her age. But if I had not been convinced before that the end of her life was nearing, I cannot ignore the facts any longer.

I keep dreaming of the cemetery in New York, of the family plot. It belongs to the Skloot family; my grandparents are there, with four of my uncles and three aunts. At the far left is my father, who has been there for forty-one years, and crammed beyond his grave, at the extreme edge, is my mother's second husband. She overrode his children's desire to have him buried beside his first wife—their mother—and was able to convince the Skloot family to squeeze him in where no outsider was intended to go. The result is that my mother's husbands now lie on either side of her waiting grave site, their headstones listing toward each other as though sharing a dark secret. Her portion of the plot is narrower than originally planned, and slightly sunken. The last time Beverly and I took my mother there, she sat on the marble bench, looked in the general direction of her husbands, and grew still. She was quiet a minute or two, and I wondered what was going through her mind. Now, in my dreams, I hear her thoughts. *When were you here last? When will you visit me again?*

All my life I have tended to deal with my mother by focusing on the immediate encounter. She was too unpredictable for any other approach. As a child, this meant watching her intently, gauging her mood, dodging her latest explosion. Later, it meant handling the current phone call, deflecting the moment's problem. I knew there was no chance I could actually do something to make her content, or change the way she acted. All that made sense was to manage each episode individually. Either that, or do what my brother did and cut off all contact. It has, I see, been easy and safe just to keep my distance from her. But now we are here together and she is only an hour's drive away.

She cannot hurt me. She is genuine in her pleasure at seeing me, her need to see me, despite the fact that she forgets immediately and does not believe I ever come. And she is dying. For both our sakes, I must begin to manage closeness with her.

We stand in her room at the end of the visit. She asks us to wait while she goes to the bathroom, till she understands when we will be back next, till she is sure we are married. As we leave the room, she fights back tears. It is no longer the happiest day of her life.

"You'll be back soon?"

"Before you know it."

# 3 Fittings

Beverly and I arrive at the nursing home shortly after noon. We enter the access code for the Memory Impairment Unit and walk down the hall to my mother's room. She is standing where she usually stands: in her bathroom, hands on the sink, gazing into the mirror, smiling at her image there.

She looks remarkable. Gone is the lacquered golden pouf, rouge, and darkened eyelids that long defined her presentation to the world. Her hair is its natural gray. It's clean and soft, and smells like human hair rather than a chemistry experiment. Instead of layers of gauzy fabric and elaborately swirled capes, she wears cotton lounging pants and an unpredictable mix of undershirts, T-shirts and sweaters. She is braless and sockless. Her feet, which have lost much of the swelling caused by a lifetime of elegant high-heeled shoes, are encased in suede sandals held in place by Velcro straps.

According to everyone involved in her care, even after a year in the nursing home my mother remains a mostly happy, jovial woman. No one has ever said that about her before. She is as transformed in spirit as in fashion. Triggered by stray words, she routinely breaks into song. Say *it's a beautiful morning, Lillian,* and she will respond by singing a few lines of Rodgers and Hammerstein about what a beautiful mornin' it is, and what a beautiful day too. Tell her there's a full moon out and she'll croon about flying her to the moon. Just don't ask her where she comes from, or where she is, or what her two husbands' names were, or what she had for lunch today.

"Do you still write?" she asks. Then adds, "Aren't you the one who writes?"

"Yes, Mother. I'm still at it."

"Then it would be nice if I ever had one of your books."

I pick up a few from her bedside table. "You've got them all."

"Oh, so nice of you to bring them at last."

I know that this little exchange is just another example of my mother's inability to form memories. She's not forgetting me or my books; she hasn't been able to place or keep them in memory. They're not there to be forgotten. Still, for all my knowing, it's frustrating to feel that our visits and our gestures offer my mother no lasting sustenance. In the most literal sense, she is oblivious to them as soon as we leave.

There is a counterbalance to that frustration: I'm amazed to hear her let go of perceived offenses so readily, to see things in a positive light. Now that dementia has ravaged her memory, she no longer hoards and seasons her indignation. This has to be as good for her as it is for me. Except for rare bursts of anger or frustration, as when she knows she cannot remember something, she seems not only cheerful but accepting, innocent, no longer expecting the worst and strategically preempting it.

As David Shenk says in his book *The Forgetting*, "When introspection begins to break down, so does willfulness." This change in my mother is almost more than I can handle. No brooding, no defensiveness or moody tirades. Who is this woman? Where was she when I was young? I wonder if this might have been my mother's "true self," hidden all along under some combination of psychological forces that I will never discover. The happy little girl buried in a rubble of wrongs. The idea fills me with sadness for her. Or perhaps my mother has truly been transformed. Perhaps her memory and the gothic theater it always housed—she never seemed to remember joy—was the very thing that tormented her. Now that memory is gone, so is the torment. Her mind seems more at ease.

And what is most on her mind now is marriage. Hers, mine, the aide's, the social worker's, the rabbi's, the TV newscaster's, the sons and daughters of her compatriots in the nursing home.

As she looks at herself in the mirror, she asks, "How old am I, dear?"

"You're nearing ninety-two."

She turns to look at me, to see if I'm joking. "Don't say such a thing." Returning her attention to the mirror, she says she hopes to find another husband soon. *The men in this place don't know what they're missing.* Then, as she still always does when we show up, she asks, "When are you two going to get married?"

I hold up my hand and let the light sparkle off my wedding ring. "We are married."

"Oh, yes." She looks back into the mirror, trying to fit the pieces together, trying to connect that image with her sense of who she is, trying to figure out how Beverly and I belong in the picture that refuses to cohere. "I remember now."

I was present when my mother, widowed five years, met the man who became her second husband. It was a New Year's Eve party in the basement of her apartment building, as 1965 turned into 1966. I'd come home for the holidays during my freshman year of college and been hired to work the party as a waiter. Minimal salary, but they said the tips would be great.

My mother's escort was an old boyfriend named Teddy, the man she'd abandoned in 1938 to marry my father. Teddy had resurfaced in her life after my father's death, first showing up as a contestant on *To Tell the Truth* in its next-to-last season. Posing as a South Seas explorer, he'd stumped Peggy Cass and Tom Poston but not Orson Bean, and made my mother stand up at the kitchen table and scream: "He's no explorer, he's Teddy Serenata!" When a grinning Teddy told Bud Collyer that he lived in New York, my mother grunted, picked up the phone, and dialed Information. She and Teddy started their second romance a week later.

By New Year's Eve, they'd been dating for over a year. I remember liking Teddy the few times I met him, a dapper little man the same size as me and my father, given to wearing striped sports jackets and loose slacks in pastel shades, his graying hair slicked back. He reminded me of the old Yankees shortstop, Phil Rizzuto. My mother said he was good company, which meant that he still wasn't husband material.

So it wasn't a surprise when my mother left that New Year's Eve party with someone else. Julius, recently widowed, was visiting his sister and brother-in-law for the holidays and had agreed to tag along with them. Fate sat them at my mother's table. By the time I served their soup, I could see what was happening.

My mother and Julius danced. Teddy sat, smiling, nodding to me or to the occasional neighbor who recognized him, growing smaller as he nibbled on a roll. My mother and Julius danced some more. He was lean and handsome, six inches taller than my mother, correct in posture, serious in demeanor. At midnight, she kissed Julius first, then pecked at Teddy's cheek and—quite publicly—the poor man was once again abandoned.

When the party broke up, Teddy left without saying good-bye, not even to me. My mother walked out arm-in-arm with her new beau, beaming. She forgot about rallying everyone to leave their waiter a tip, and I ended up with five dollars from the table for my night's work. They were married in early March.

"Yes, I remember when you met," my mother says now, walking over to us. "I was there. Some kind of party. Floyd, you came with somebody else, what's-her-name, your old girlfriend, the Italian. Then you met beautiful Beverly. You forgot the Italian immediately and out you walked with this one. Very romantic."

That is, of course, not how Beverly and I met. But such confabulations are typical of the way memory and identity and time have grown fluid for my mother now. She might say, *Oh Floyd, it's so good to see you. How is your house on the lake?* (this is addressed to her late brother, whose house on Lake Mahopac in New York was a place she last visited about thirty years ago). *I'm glad you stopped with the cigars* (to my father, who died in 1961). *Let's go up to my room later, and don't forget to bring me a*

*Pepsi* (this is to Irv, her final boyfriend, whom she last saw in New York about a year ago).

I'm trying to learn how to drift in time with her, to let go of my yearning for a genuine conversation or connection, for the things she says to make sense. If I can do that, it becomes possible to witness her rediscovery of things I've never known about. Suddenly, there's a touch of warmth in these stray memories, and a veracity that convinces me they're real. Passing a friendly Weimaraner and her owner as we approached a coffee shop, I expected her to recoil and curse the man for exposing her to potential filth. Instead, she said, *Oh, what a nice doggie!* and stopped, hands lifting from her walker, to add, *We had a dog when I was a little girl. Its name was Wee-toy but Papa called it Pee-toy because it always wet the carpet.* Huh? My mother had a dog? In a Bronx apartment? It peed and wasn't immediately put to sleep?

Mostly, though, her memory fails utterly. When two students from Portland State University, as part of their course requirements, visited the nursing home on a strangely ironic mission to help residents compile "memory books," they were unable to discover anything from my mother except that her parents sold furs in New York. She simply could not tell them anything about her life. The problem, in part, was that they asked directly. My mother can't retrieve items from memory that way anymore; they have to surface of their own accord, driftwood on a sea of forgetfulness. And she certainly can't present her few memories in any sort of coherent whole—she can't tell a story now, can't connect the few bits that remain into a narrative. So, when asked, she didn't remember her marriages, her relatives, her experiences in art or theater, her childhood. She did think she had a son who was a writer. But he died. One of the students called me to schedule a visit here, to collect photographs and assemble a life story.

"Your mother is so sweet," she said. "She didn't remember anything, but she kept asking me if I was married and if my husband was kind to me."

We've learned that our visits create agitation in my mother unless we take her on an outing. If we stay at the nursing home with her, if she feels that she must host us, things deteriorate quickly. Like a child welcoming adults to her room, she will show us her bed, the clothes in her closet, her bathroom. But it's apparent that she doesn't recognize much, and isn't sure whose things she's finding. She will grab a photograph off her bureau and get confused over the image. She will point to the armchair we bought when she moved to the nursing home and announce that it's been in her family for years. Then she will come to a halt, look around her in alarm, race into the bathroom and, after a brief tinkle, stand in front of the mirror for a while. If we walk with her to the nursing home's plush lobby or to the solarium at the end of her unit, places where "visits" happen, she gets tangled in loops of failed conversation and grows increasingly confused.

"Your girlfriend is gorgeous," she will say. "You two should get married."

"We are married."

"You are? For how long?"

"Almost ten years."

"Ten years? Was I at the wedding?"

"No. You were still living in New York then, and you felt it was too far for you to travel."

"I lived in New York?"

"For over ninety years."

She will shake her head. "You two should get married already."

Social interaction and conversation may wear my mother down, but trips in the car still delight her. Starbucks is still a reliable destination. When we arrive, she says, *This is my favorite restaurant. Let's come here for my birthday.* People smile as she makes her way inside and stops to look around. Within the gate of her walker, she beams and waves like Harry Truman at a whistle stop, pleased with the welcome she's receiving. Best of all are errands, when there's something the resident care manager has suggested that we purchase for my mother. We spent two hours with her selecting those sandals she loves, an hour in a drugstore examining eyebrow pencils. She wasn't sure she needed one, since she'd started using a #2 pencil and had plenty of those.

During a quarterly care meeting with the nursing home staff, we got a note saying that my mother needed bras. When she'd first arrived at the home in late winter, the nurses welcoming my mother told us she would be much happier without a bra. They gave us the old, tattered one she'd been wearing and said they couldn't wait for the day when they could trash their own as well. Now, though, as she is helped to dress in the mornings, my mother apparently wonders where her bras went. She forgets about it once her shirt is on, but a recent rash under her breasts seems to have convinced everyone that she could use a bra after all.

Beverly asked her hospice colleagues where the best place was to take an elderly woman for a proper fitting. The advice was unanimous: Victoria's Secret. So we took her to the mall.

We planned this outing to coincide with a visit from California by my late brother's wife, Elaine. Though my mother remembered neither Elaine nor my brother, she was elated to have an extra visitor, and we felt the need for an extra female helper. Elaine, who had been volunteering at a shop where breast cancer survivors were fitted for their bras, brought her special expertise to this project.

At Victoria's Secret, a young woman greeted my mother warmly. "Hello! I'm Jenny and I'm here to help you!"

"Good," my mother said, blinking at all the lights and colors. "I'll take one of each."

Jenny smiled and said, "We can put you into anything you like. And in any style or any color. We could even do hot pink."

"That's very nice, dear. What's hot pink?"

As we made our slow way to the back of the shop, my mother—probably in response to seeing all the lingerie—asked, "How many husbands did I have?"

"Two, Mother. There was my father Harry, and then there was Julius."

She shakes her head, stops, leans her weight onto her walker, and I can see she's trying to figure something out. She points toward Beverly and Elaine, who are working together within the racks, gathering a selection of bras. "I'm just trying to remember who those lovely women are. I'm going through the alphabet: A for Al, no, that was my brother; B for Beverly: that's right, Beverly, the one on the right there, she's your daughter; C for, for, Charles, I think I had a cousin named Charles. Where is he?" She looks around the shop, then adds, "Or maybe I was married to a Charles. I don't know. D? E for everyone," and she stops, utterly lost. Elaine's name doesn't come up.

I lead her toward the fitting room. Beverly and Elaine have several bras ready for my mother, who looks at them, looks down, and says, "How did I get such a big bazoom?" Then she goes into the room with her two daughters-in-law, and the door is shut. "Stay right there," she calls to me, as though I were six and apt to get lost.

I take a seat in the small nook between changing rooms, holding my mother's walker folded in my lap with my cane across the top to keep it in place. I look very small. Behind doors to my left, a woman is trying on panties, dropping the unsatisfactory ones in a small pile at her feet. I don't know where to turn my eyes.

Amid the laughter and murmuring from inside my mother's changing room, I can tell that things are not going well. Nothing fits, not even close. Elaine exits, returns in a moment with another armful. It's like a skit from *I Love Lucy*, underwear in mounds all around. Jenny keeps bringing new models back to the changing room; she has a thong draped over her forearm, and I'm relieved to see her hand it to the customer in the room to my left. Jenny is losing hope and interest. Apparently, Victoria's Secret can't offer its brand of support to anyone larger than a 38.

"Try the Lane Bryant shop at the other end of the mall," she says, and I race ahead to procure a wheelchair for my mother. This is going to take longer than we'd thought.

After a stop at the rest room, we're all relieved to discover that Lane Bryant has what my mother needs. It takes about a half hour of trying on various models, but she is pleased.

"I'm so lucky to have my two daughters with me," my mother says at one point. "But who is that man right outside the door, sitting in a wheelchair?"

We buy two bras, and she leaves the store wearing one. Within thirty seconds, as we move toward the rest rooms again, my mother is squirming in the chair, reaching around to adjust her bra, and complaining about the fit.

"We'll take them back after you go to the bathroom."

"Stupid brassiere."

Back at Lane Bryant, my mother has run out of patience. Nothing fits. Bras dangle over the top of the changing room door. Elaine, ever cheerful, has found something in every size, shape, and style, but always the fit is wrong.

"That's enough," my mother finally says. "Just give me the bra I came in and take me to the hotel."

Beverly comes flying out of the changing room. "Now we're in trouble," she says. In a flash, she's returned with the perfect bra, larger where all the others were too small and smaller where they were too large.

"Is this the one I came in?"

"Do you like it?"

"Of course. That's why I always wear it."

After one more bathroom stop, we leave the mall. My mother is tired but smiling. As I drive, she takes a deep breath, looks out her window, and listens for a moment to the quiet discussion happening in the back seat. "Excuse me," she says, "who are those nice women behind us?"

For more than twenty years, neurologists have recognized the phenomenon of retrogenesis at work in Alzheimer's patients. The sequence of their functional losses reverses the sequence of functional gains in childhood development. They lose their capacities in precisely the opposite order in which they gained them—the ability to hold up their heads, to smile, crawl, walk, control their bowels, their urine, to dress themselves—are removed in inverse order.

This harrowing pattern is obvious in my mother's case. Her dementia has been progressing and capacities regressing in the classic manner. She sounds like my mother—her smoky contralto voice and New York accent are for me instantly resonant with memories—but she is essentially functioning as a seven-year-old child. She is not quite able to select proper clothing or put it all on without assistance, is unable to prepare a meal or handle simple finances, is still continent but not fully reliable when bathing alone. Her voice will suddenly alter, rising into an unfamiliar range when she whines or pleads, offering good behavior in return for a treat. It is a grim, frightening process to witness, and I am trying to see the situation for what it is: a gradual letting go. For me as well as for my mother, as she steadily releases hold on herself and her world.

She also exhibits some of the charming naiveté of a seven-year-old. When we tell her we're taking her for a ride, her eyes widen, her hands come up to the sides of her face and she says, *Oh goodie! A ride.* She is open to experience, at least in the moment it occurs; everything seems fresh to her and filled with wonder. There is little of the adult or even adolescent irony in the presence of simple goodness, so that when she sees a couple holding hands in Starbucks she is charmed. *What nice looking people. I wonder if they're married.* In the past, their mixture of races and discrepancy in ages would have brought immediate censure. Her skepticism has diminished along with her cognitive hold; there are flickers of simple genuine joy that are astonishing to behold. She is trusting and she is elemental. She often feels relieved of great burdens, pleased not to worry about managing her hair or having her fancy clothes dry cleaned. *I don't have to do that anymore.*

The things that she does worry about, such as when I will return or when I last visited, seem most often connected to my presence: I worry her. I am her chief source of agitation. But the form of her worry no longer is that of a mother for a son. Rather, she worries as a child worries about its father.

When will I be there again, what have I brought for her, how long will I stay, when will I leave?

Still, for all her childlike qualities, my mother is quite obviously ninety-one-plus. There is no ignoring her thin parchment skin, her limited vision, diminishing mobility, dementia. She is shrinking in body as well as consciousness, fading before our eyes. I try to think of her situation as a liberation, since her lifelong sense of disappointment caused her such misery and now she appears so content. But the idea of liberation keeps transforming into imprisonment; she is a child trapped in an old woman's body and just at the point where she might finally feel free she is losing hold of herself. No wonder she is compelled to gaze at what remains in the mirror.

This time in our life is a labyrinth of role reversals and reorientations. I feel both protective and frustrated, the way I often felt as a young father. But there is also a long, dark shadow of history that comes with being in my mother's presence, with being her sole surviving son, her only surviving connection to a past she no longer remembers and I cannot forget.

As we leave her room, my mother stands in the hallway trying to make her impressions fit. She is perched between the rails of her walker, one hand raised to wave goodbye, the other stretched as though to stop us. Her tone alternates between pleasure and panic. *This was the happiest day of my life! Wait, I have to go to the bathroom! You're coming back in how many days? Bring one of your books already. Marry that girl.*

# 4  The Melody Lingers On

As her dementia deepens, it's clear that my mother no longer remembers her life. Thoughts drift as though in zero gravity, bumping occasionally against a few stray bits of memory, but nothing holds still. Her family and the long-time community acquaintances who filled her days, her ambitions and achievements, her travels and yearnings—almost everything has floated away from her grasp, mere debris.

"Was I happily married?" she asked last week, when Beverly and I took her out for coffee and snacks. Before I could answer, she added, "*Oh how we somethinged on the hmmm hmm we were wed.* Dear, was I ever on the stage?"

I nodded and said, "On the radio, too."

"I was on the radio?" She smiled, closed her eyes, and sang "*Birds gotta swim, fish gotta fly, da-dada-da one man da-da die.*" Then she lifted a fragment of blueberry muffin and said, "Was I ever on the stage?"

It's not just her distant past that's gone. What happened two minutes ago is as lost as what happened during the twenty-seven years she lived in Manhattan, the twenty years she lived in Brooklyn, or the forty-four years she lived on Long Island. Now that she's in Oregon, she doesn't know she ever lived elsewhere. Sometimes she believes her Portland nursing home is a Long Island beachfront hotel, just as she sometimes believes I am her late brother.

What's become apparent, though, is that she still knows songs. She retains many lyrics, snatches that may get confused but are easily recognizable, and when the lyrics are missing the melodies remain. She loves to sing, sings on key and with zest, and I can't help wondering why song has hung on so tenaciously while her life memories have not.

It's tempting to take the psychological approach: she never was very happy with her life, but she was happy dreaming of stardom as a torch singer. She was happy knowing she'd had a brief career singing on radio in the mid-1930s, where her five-minute program on WBNX in the Bronx aired opposite Rudy Vallee. In the chemical bath of her mind, she always trans-formed a few years of apprentice costume work in the legiti-mate theater, and an assortment of roles in local community theater, into a protracted career *In the Thee-aye-tre*. No question: she loved performing. I remember how extravagantly she ac-companied herself on the piano, sliding along the bench to reach her notes, stomping the pedals, rising and sitting again, going through her brief repertoire before erupting with gusto at the end as a signal for applause. According to this psycho-logical approach, my mother forgets what she needs to forget, and is left with song.

But such an explanation isn't really convincing, not when the evidence of deep organic brain damage is so apparent in her activities of daily living. She cannot dress herself, needs reminding during a meal if she is to continue eating, can-not process new information. Her failures of memory are not choices, not driven by subconscious needs. It must be that, unlike personal memories or the recall of facts, such things as song lyrics are stored in a part of her brain that has, so far, escaped the ravages of her dementia.

As a result of advances in neuroscience, the pattern of my mother's losses can be pinpointed biologically. First, there's the sheer diminishment in her overall cognitive capacity. At the rate brain mass normally shrinks during our sixties and sev-enties, my mother's brain has probably lost about a quarter of its size by now. In addition, as Daniel L. Schacter says in *Search-ing for Memory*, in normal aging "blood flow and uptake of oxy-gen both decrease significantly" and there is "widespread loss of neurons in the cortex," a major site of memory storage. In

Alzheimer's patients, the shrinking brain also becomes clotted with plaques and tangles, and there is further neuron loss in the hippocampus, a part of the brain associated with the ability to remember the on-going incidents in our lives. This set of compounding pathologies explains most of her symptoms, but not the curious endurance of those songs. It's most likely that my mother's lifelong joy in performing, and the powerful emotional forces associated with it for her, have enabled the deeper storage of lyric and melody in her amygdala. This almond-shaped organ in the inner brain is critical for forming and sustaining emotional memories. Though most often spoken of in connection with persistent, enduring traumatic memories, it also is responsible for enduring positive memories. This is where our most vivid memories reside, etched there by a mix of chemical and physical processes that ensure their endurance. I suspect that my mother's amygdala has not yet been overtaken by her disease process. This would explain not only the persistence of her song repertoire, but the relative calmness and sweetness she still manifests. As David Shenk notes in *The Forgetting*, when the "amygdala becomes compromised, control over primitive emotions like fear, anger, and craving is disrupted; hostile emotions and bursts of anxiety may occur all out of proportion to events, or even out of nowhere."

My mother is not there yet. In trying to reduce her symptoms to these objective clinical explanations, I know I'm trying to cushion myself from the changes she's undergone and from what lies ahead. But this is my mother, not some interesting case history in a neurology text. This is the woman who fought to allow my birth, eight years after my older brother's, overcoming my father's continuing resistance. The woman who recited nonsense verse to me, based on a traditional Chinese chain tale, sounds I still remember fifty years later though she does not: *Nicky nicky tembo, whatso rembo, wudda wudda boosky, hippo pendro, national pom pom.* The woman, so miserable and disappointed throughout her life, filled with anger, volatile, friendless in old age, who now in dementia has grown sweet and accommodating, happy to greet the day, who has come back to song.

Those songs of hers, which routinely interrupt any effort at communication, are in fact signs of hope. They represent an enduring part of her past, connected with the rare joy in her life, which is why they linger when so much is gone. I must learn to welcome rather than be annoyed by them. In many ways, they're all we have left of her.

Like the mass of her brain, the physical structure of my mother's body is also shrinking. At her tallest, about 5'1", the top of her head used to be level with the middle of my forehead; now she comes up to my throat. She was always wide, too, a solid and blocky woman whose flowing outfits didn't disguise her figure as she'd hoped. She took up room despite being small. But now she has lost both water and mass. Her once swollen legs have slimmed; she sags and looks frail. It's as though my mother is pulling herself in around a diminishing core, the dwindling autobiographical self she's losing touch with, and closing down before my eyes.

She was moving slowly toward our table in the coffee shop, inching her walker along, taking a few steps and stopping. When she reached the table where Beverly was placing napkins and spoons, she looked around with a smile, let go of her side rails, tilted her head heavenward and sang, *La wonderful, da marvelous, la da da.*

Her voice still comes from down near her chest, the way it's supposed to, a richly resonating smoky contralto. It's almost as deep as my own off-key tenor. But as a young singer, my mother was a soprano. There are three surviving 78 RPM records from her radio show that prove it. George Gershwin was alive when my mother was "The Melody Girl of the Air," and Gershwin was her favorite. There were times when she hinted at a romance with him, never going quite so far as to say they'd dated, but implying that a certain dashing young composer—whom she was not at liberty to name but who had a dowdy lyricist brother—was once very interested in her.

Her solid fifty years of unfiltered Chesterfields transformed my mother's voice and, though she stopped smoking in her early seventies, those cigarettes remain audible now in her gravelly tones. But she can and does still belt out the tunes, holding nothing back. This dynamic and deeper voice is how I remember her singing. I never could make sense out of those old records, the high pitched girlishness, the piercing delivery. In my hearing, she sang dark and windy.

There was always a well-tuned mahogany piano against a living room wall in our various apartments. Its lid was shut, its music desk empty, its surfaces without dust or fingerprints. No one was allowed to sit on its bench or open the keyboard lid, much less touch the keys or press the pedals down. No examining the sheet music hidden inside the bench. She wasn't sure she wanted us even to *look* at the piano.

By the 1950s, as I was growing up, my mother's performance repertoire had been condensed to five tunes that she would play in the same order. She seldom sang more than one refrain and chorus, took no requests, brooked no singing along. She would consent to entertain at the end of small dinner parties or holiday meals, perching on the bench and holding her chin up until there was total silence. Then she struck a chord *fortissimo* and launched herself into performance. First came the Gershwin portion of the program, "They Can't Take That Away From Me," "'S Wonderful," and "Our Love Is Here to Stay." Then she did Rodgers and Hart's "Bewitched, Bothered and Bewildered" from *Pal Joey* and finished with her signature song, Jerome Kern and Oscar Hammerstein's "Can't Help Lovin' Dat Man," from *Show Boat.* No encores. She was still, it seemed, tied to the fifteen-minute radio show format.

I see now that her songs were songs of love, joyful love. Along with fame as a performer, this was the other great unfulfilled yearning of her life. It was not there with the man she married first, the man she spoke of in my hearing as "your father the butcher." Nor was it there apparently with her second husband, a kind and gentle widower, the man she spoke of as "that nice, handsome fellow." After his death, when she moved into a retirement hotel overlooking the boardwalk, my mother had a succession of boyfriends but none without glaring faults—too old and bent, too devoted to children and grandchildren, too working-class, too senile. Now, from within her own dementia, one of the main themes woven through her rambling speech is love, joyful love. Was she happily married? Does she have a boyfriend? Are Beverly and I married? Are we happy? Is the nurse married? The young man behind the Starbucks counter? Can we help my mother find a new boyfriend?

Even as a child, I sensed something that made me very uncomfortable with my mother's recitals. It wasn't just the showy way she played, or the too-familiar spontaneity of her moves. It had to do with the look on her face, a rapturous hunger, and the sudden exposure of her deepest, most obsessive wishes. She leaped off her piano bench like a nearly drowned diver suddenly bursting to the surface, head back, mouth wide open, and I imagine her longing was palpable to everyone. There was something brazenly sad about her selection of romantic hits, a sadness I failed to appreciate for most of my life. She must have wanted what she could never have, what few people ever have, and she hadn't let go of the need: idealized romantic love. Her play list was a litany of failed dreams.

Those failed dreams and her overall sense of disgruntlement seem to have shrunk now too. With the fading of memory and life story has come an apparent narrowing of mood. From the outside, seeing how she is now, this phenomenon suggests a compensation for her shattering losses, and I hope that's how it works for her. I know it could have been otherwise. Like so many people with Alzheimer's or deep dementia, she could long ago have become even angrier and more tormented, hostile and restless.

My mother looked down at the coffee in her cup, unsure what to do with it. She gazed into its tawny surface and blinked. Only when she looked away did she, as though triggered by signals from a more instinctive zone of her brain, lift the cup toward her lips. I helped her steady it.

"Was I ever on the stage, dear?" she asked again.

I responded automatically, singing the opening phrase of "I Whistle a Happy Tune" from *The King and I*, and she beamed, picking up the tune itself, humming along, nodding firmly. One way to look at this, I've realized, is to consider song lyrics as my mother's native tongue. Tonal and melodious, its beauties of sound offset by the banality of its linguistic content. Well, beauties of sound when she sings it, not when I do.

"What comes next?" she asked.

I give her the line and she nods again, taking over, finishing out the sentence after her own fashion: *so no one da dee da I forget.*

From the mid-1950s to the mid-1970s, my mother was active in community theater. She was usually cast in small singing roles. I remember her playing Melba Snyder in *Pal Joey*, doing the strip-tease number "Zip" in the basement of our Brooklyn synagogue. She played the nanny in *Auntie Mame*, where she was dressed up by Mame and her friend Vera for one night as a swinger and sang a song about finally having lived. She was King Mongkut's first wife, Lady Thiang, in *The King and I*, shunted aside for younger wives, the romance of marriage gone though she still admires her husband and tells Anna so ("Something Wonderful"). Taking on a non-singing role, she was Yente the Matchmaker in *Fiddler on the Roof*. What these roles all have in common is their tangential relationship to passion: a cynical stripper, an unglamorous nanny spruced up for a quick taste of the sexy high life, a queen spurned and settling for grandeur instead of romance, an old woman whose business is brewing love for others. Ironically, even as she got to fulfill her desire for performing, the roles she played reenacted romantic failure and disappointment.

I performed with her on occasion, when no reasonable excuse could be found. When she was in *The King and I*, I was ten and played one of the King's children, learning my small schoolroom speech ("What is that green over there?"), rehearsing the March of the Siamese Children, singing in my brief solo about being bright and breezy. At thirteen, during a horrifying cabaret-style local fund-raiser, I sang a duet with her, the dutiful Sonny Boy climbing upon my mother's knee though we were the same size.

When she wasn't part of a play's cast, she still became engaged in the productions. She attended rehearsals to play the piano or read cues or kibbitz. She painted sets. Resorting to her earliest contributions to the theater, she helped design costumes.

I remember her working on hat designs for a production of *Guys and Dolls*. She would glue buttons onto blank greeting cards, paint black dots for eyes in the buttonholes and red dots for mouths, add a few ink strokes for hair. Then she snipped bits of fabric and feathers to resemble hats, pasted them onto the crowns of the buttons and made tiny adjustments with toothpicks. Below the buttons, she drew the shape of necks, then added scarves or ties. It was possible for her to devote four or five intense hours a night to this work, cigarettes smoldering in her abalone shell ashtray. The finished illustrations would be spread out over a card table to dry or for further modification. Finally, she would bring them to rehearsal, stacked in a shoe box, and get herself ready for another round.

My mother was, clearly, a trouper. I cannot remember her being as focused or as sprightly as she was at her design work or within the acting company. She saved all the reviews from our local paper, all the programs, and most of the scripts. I found them in a storage locker when she moved into the retirement hotel and, just glancing at them, felt myself swamped with the scents and sounds of her theatrical life.

As we turned onto Boundary Avenue, bringing my mother back to the nursing home after our outing, Beverly said, "This is the street where you live."

Then, as though on cue, all three of us started singing Lerner and Loewe's "On the Street Where You Live." My mother's voice fractured into laughter and she could hardly keep singing. Besides, she didn't exactly have the words anymore. So she went into scat: *I have doo doo do, la da dee doo da, knowing I'm doo be la where you live.* We pulled up to the front door, all three of us cackling at our mutual cleverness.

I've noticed during recent visits that my mother's repertoire has actually expanded. She's no longer limited to the Big Five Hits. Now she'll bring out songs I never heard her sing before, like "Fly Me to the Moon" or "Anything Goes," which I recognize from the sustained melodies more than from the snippet of lyrics she can muster. Dixon and Henderson's "Bye, Bye Blackbird" from 1926, Gus Kahn's "Makin' Whoopee" from 1928. She sings Yiddish songs too, all new to me, songs she must have learned during her childhood, when Yiddish was spoken at home and in the Upper West Side neighborhoods where she lived. I haven't heard her speak a word of Yiddish since we moved from Brooklyn in 1957 and cannot remember her ever singing in the language that might have marked her as marginal. She also now has the melodies for some Hebrew tunes she must be picking up during Sabbath services at the nursing home. I don't believe they come from her memory tune-bank because she never went to the synagogue except for social or theatrical events, and I haven't heard her utter a word in Hebrew before.

Much as I'm amazed to hear her dredge up songs from her childhood or youth, it's the phenomenon of new songs—"Adon Olam," for instance, and "Hatikvah"—that astounds me. Perhaps this means that, because she still connects so powerfully to music, she can somehow learn and remember fresh material, at least song material, particularly melodies, though in conversation she cannot remember the question she asked a moment before, or whether we told her what state we live in, or if we're married. Asked if she has been to Sabbath services, she says, "No, they don't have them here." But they do, and she has, and the melodies have stuck.

She also comes up with songs I know she's heard in my lifetime, but I hadn't realized she remembered. And she delivers them with genuine glee. *Be down to la da in a taxi do dee, doo dah be-dee dee in your hay dee hay.* Gradually, I've been discovering that this is an opportunity for conversation of a sort. While it's not possible for me to ask her questions and get meaningful answers, or share information with her about the life Beverly and I are leading, or even go over memories of childhood with her, we can approximate the give and take of conversation through song. "What are those?" I'll say, pointing to the necklace of beads she's made during a crafts session. "Baubles? Bangles?" And she'll say, *Bubbles, Bingles, light something beads la da dee dah.* Or I'll hum the opening notes from "If I Were a Rich Man" and she will pick up the song from there.

I'm beginning to find a solace in this exchange. We have the rhythm of conversation, if not the content. A form of give and take that enables us still to feel connected by words, or at least by meaningful sounds. "The song is ended," as her favorite songwriter wrote, "but the melody lingers on." We are holding on to the melody of contact. And they can't take that away from me, from us, at least not yet.

# part two  *A Pick to the Heart*

# 5  1957

To enter the nursing home's Memory Impairment Unit, I press a four-digit code on a keypad beside the locked door. It is an easy number for me to remember: *1957*. 1957 was the year my family moved from Brooklyn to another world, a small barrier island off the south shore of Long Island. It was the year the Dodgers, my favorite team, moved from Brooklyn to another world too. They became the Los Angeles Dodgers, transplanting a team named for the Brooklyn phenomenon of dodging trolleys and pretending they could be the same in the vast spaces of 1957 Los Angeles. Fittingly, 1957 was the year Brooklyn's trolleys ceased. And Oliver Hardy, and the Hudson Hornet. The air was full of threat in 1957: Asian flu, Sputnik, alien abductions in Brazil. I was ten, and what happened in the world for the first time truly seemed to reverberate inside our family, to be deeply personal. I recognized a confluence of endings, relocations, and dangers. 1957 was the last year my father was whole, before an automobile accident crushed his legs in 1958 and led irrevocably to his death three years later. 1957 was the year my mother reached the peak of her powers, uprooting us all in a quixotic quest for privilege and elegance. My brother lost his way in 1957, suddenly cut off at age eighteen from lifelong friends and familiar territory, and my system of immune defenses first began revealing its flaws.

So events from that year remain etched in my memory despite brain damage and long-term memory loss. I do not forget the code to the Memory Impairment Unit. I might forget where Beverly and I are going as we drive the hour east into

Portland to see my mother, or what we had for breakfast shortly before leaving home, or the three-digit code to erase messages from our new telephone answering machine on which I have just heard my daughter's voice, or her phone number in her Manhattan apartment. But I remember *1957*.

The last time Beverly and I visited my mother, she no longer quite knew who we were. But she was very happy to see us.

We found her sitting at her usual table in the western corner of the solarium, facing a view of oak and maple trees she cannot actually see because of her shattered vision. She had just finished a snack drink and was contemplating the straw when we greeted her with kisses and sat on either side of her.

"Oh, oh," she said, clasping her hands beneath her chin. She looked closely at me, bringing the image together. "You're my, you're, I, you're a Relative!"

I explained who we were, that I was her son and Beverly was my wife, that my father was Harry, the butcher who died in 1961, that she had grown up in Manhattan where her parents operated a fur business, and had lived in New York all her life until two years ago when we moved her to Oregon.

"But how do I look?" she asked when I finished.

"Beautiful," Beverly said, taking my mother's hand. "Your skin is amazing."

My mother looked down at the two enfolded hands and said, "I don't have a boyfriend though."

"You still might find one," I said.

She turned her gaze back in my direction. "Your voice is very familiar. Can you find a boyfriend for me?"

"I think that might be your job."

She nodded. "I don't want any butchers, though." There was a pause, then she withdrew her hand from Beverly's, looked at it, and said, "How old am I?"

"Well, I'm fifty-five," I told her. "So how old do you think you are?"

She leaned close to me again, studied my face, and said,

"Forty-five?" I lifted my hand and flicked the fingers upwards. "Sixty?" More flicking. "Seventy?"

"You're ninety-two."

She looked down, closed her eyes, shook her head. "No wonder I don't have a boyfriend."

We talked for a while about how pretty she looked, and about how well the beaded jewelry she made went with her clothes.

"Excuse me, dear," my mother said. "But who was I married to?"

"Well, your first husband was Harry Skloot."

"That's you!"

"No, that was my father. I'm Floyd Skloot."

"You're Floyd Skloot?"

My mother's voice softened toward a whisper. It was hard to hear her because a woman at the next table was issuing instructions to an auditorium full of imaginary students. At least I think that's what she was doing. Her tone was peremptory, her rhythm singsong, and her voice projected like an actress' toward the cheap balcony seats, the way my mother spoke on stage in her heyday. But this woman was speaking in nonsense syllables. Her gibberish filled the solarium like the early spring sunlight

"That's right," my mother was saying. "Of course. Because I was your father."

In 1957, my mother was forty-seven years old and ready for a new life. She had actually been ready for a new life since 1926, when she was sixteen and sensed that reality was failing to live up to her expectations. Where, for example, was Rudolph Valentino, whom she had been hoping to hear from for the last few years? Newly dead, that's where. Another matrimonial candidate removed from the scene. And where was her invitation to perform at Carnegie Hall? Her discovery by a Broadway producer? Her opening at the new Valentine Gallery, which was showing all the modern European art? If things had gone according to plan, Valentine would have staged an exhibit of her work, she would have met and married the man's partner—Pierre Matisse—and moved to Paris. Nothing was working out right.

What I know about my mother's early years is fragmentary. I believe that's what she always intended. There was a core of often repeated stories: her mama and papa were furriers whose clients were all from Paris Budapest Prague Madrid; she quit public school at fourteen in order to study art; she attended her cousin Helen's wedding in Belgium in 1928, meeting a ravishing Count Duke Earl Baron; she went to work for a costume company in the theater district. Somewhere in there, she had her radio program opposite Rudy Vallee. All along, she was courted *by men of the highest caliber*. Then she was twenty-eight and married my father.

There was apparently little else to share with a son who kept asking for details. She would look down, allow a small smile, and shake her head, implying that it was all too wonderful and exotic to be discussed, too complicated and astonishing for a son to grasp. Or too disappointing to speak of. I understood early that her past was equal parts haut monde fantasies and harsh fiasco; I assembled from scraps and attitude a fractured narrative of her past. All I knew for sure was she was unsatisfied with life's performance so far.

As I reached the age of ten, I feared that our two-bedroom apartment in East Flatbush could not contain the family any longer. We were no more crowded than before, but were being squeezed out by unseen forces. It was just my parents, my older brother, and me, but mushrooming rages seemed to swell the air of the place like a highly flammable gas. There were explosions of serious violence.

My brother, graduating from high school in June, did not want to go to college and my parents were furious. They would throw him out! They would not support him unless he was in school! He was not equipped to do anything! Night after night, over dinner, the same angry exchange as my brother tried to eat and get away: *What are you going to do with your life? I don't know.* I remember seeing my father suddenly erupt at the table and backhand my brother, sending his forkful of green peas flying around the room, which made my mother scream about the mess, which made me get down and begin picking individual peas off the floor, which made my brother kick me like a football.

My father's entire adult life had been devoted to owning and operating a live, Kosher poultry market on Union Street. Now he was facing the end of its viability. Every night, in the two hours between his arrival home and his going to sleep, he barked about supermarkets that were putting retail markets like his out of business, expressways that would cut the waterfront district off from the rest of Brooklyn, the Mafia horning in, the increase in rent from the building's owners—his mother and brother. *What am I supposed to do, work for the A&P?*

My mother was, she said, fed up. Fed up with living in a small apartment in a stupid middle class neighborhood, with mundane rundown shops and crowded stinking buses and all her friends moving to ritzy Long Island and no one left to appreciate her too-long-ignored artistic side. Her children, the big *trombenik* who was good-for-nothing and the little *pisher* who knows nothing about anything, were destroying her life. It was all more than she could stand and time was passing them by. She was talking about a return to the stage, a real home to decorate in high style, a life of finer things before it was too late.

There was a rumor that the building we lived in would be sold to the state of New York for conversion to student dormitories when the new medical school was finished across the street. My mother wanted my father to sell his market, since it was doomed anyway, and go to work for her brother.

"He makes ladies' clothes, for Christ's sake," my father said, pointing his dinner knife at her from across the table. "I'm a goddamn butcher."

My mother folded her arms, closed her eyes, and said, "And I, my dear, should never have been a butcher's wife."

I press *1957*, Beverly opens the door, and we walk down a long hall toward the solarium. We pass my mother's room, a photograph of her face with its vacant stare posted beside the door.

My mother is seldom in her room. Tormented more and more by dementia's timeless chaos, she is increasingly anxious about where she is supposed to go or what she is supposed to do. She is calm only when among others, though she has no idea who they might be and does not interact with them. Being with others lets her know she is, at least, somewhere. When there are musical activities or entertainments in the nursing home, when there are lectures or discussion groups or outings, she will still be led out of the Memory Impairment Unit and do well within the nursing home's general population. Provided an aide arrives in time to lead her back when the event is finished. She still loves to sing, and accompanies all visiting performers whether invited to or not.

The rest of her time is spent in the solarium, which is where we are heading when we pass my mother's room and our attention is caught by a flurry of activity inside. With my mother always out and her roommate, devastated by stroke damage, unable to move or speak, we are used to passing a still, silent space where my mother dwells. We enter on occasion, only to check her things and be sure there is nothing she needs.

Now there must be ten people in the room. They cluster to the left of the entrance, standing around the roommate's bed, talking, murmuring. Beverly and I look at each other. We have never seen visitors in the room before and cannot imagine how my mother would respond to such a crowd. The only thing we can be sure of is that she is not in there.

She is at her table in the solarium, pen in her hand, scrawling faces on page after page of scratch paper. The faces are skimpier versions of the aristocratic women she used to sketch, slender faces with bright red pursed lips, haughtily wide eyes and elaborate hats. Now the faces are elongated and lopsided as though viewed in a funhouse mirror. Eyes are mere dots, lips swoop like birds in flight and there are no hats, just wisps that suggest hair. Or feathers.

"Hello, Mother." We bend over to kiss her, then sit. "It's Floyd and Beverly. Good to see you."

She looks at me and reaches out with her right hand, pen first. I am not sure if she intends to draw in a better nose or has forgotten the pen altogether. But she cups her fingers and strokes my cheek with her knuckles.

"You have a beard?"

"Yes. For the last thirty-three years."

She nods at me and says, "I know who you are now. You're Beverly."

"How do you feel?" I ask.

"All right. Except I have nowhere to live."

"What do you mean? You live here."

"Somebody else is in my room." She shakes her head. "They took away my home. I'll have to move, I guess."

Beverly understands what she means before I do. "You aren't moving, Mother. Those people in your room are just visiting your roommate."

"My roommate? Nonsense. I would never have a room-mate."

We shift the conversation toward safer ground, telling her she looks well, her jewelry is lovely, it's wonderful to see her. But she is shaking her head, looking grim.

"Where do you live?" she asks.

"In a small town called Amity. It's about an hour from here."

"Amity? You came all that way to see me?"

"It's no problem."

"If I moved to your house, you wouldn't have to drive so far."

"I know. But our house is too small. There's barely room for us. And it's in the woods."

My mother continues to shake her head and frown. "Who lives in the woods?"

I don't answer, knowing she's talking to herself, but am impressed by how tenaciously she is holding onto this topic.

"I know what," she says. "I'll buy you a new house on the Upper West Side and we can all move together."

What I remember most vividly from the year 1957 is a bowl of chicken-and-rice soup. It sat steaming before me on the afternoon of Tuesday, October 15, the day we moved from Brooklyn. I had a temperature of 104 degrees, a hacking cough, and could not swallow without pain. Typical symptoms of a potent influenza virus.

The 1957 Asian flu pandemic killed over a million people worldwide and sickened more than half of America's schoolchildren. It had spread from Japan and Singapore in May, causing scattered outbreaks through summer, then went wild when classrooms opened in autumn. It was one of those strains that emerge when avian and human influenza mix together in swine, causing a so-called antigenic shift, an essentially new virus that is therefore masked to human immune systems.

I remember feeling sicker than ever in my life, moving in and out of delirium, confused about where I was. My bedroom wallpaper seemed animated and strange, its flowers dancing as though in wind and clustering into the sneering shapes of gargoyles' faces. There was a noise in my head that I took to be the sound of ocean waves from near our new home. But at the same time, our old apartment was being packed up around me as I lay in bed. We had so much stuff that my father said it would take the movers a month just to load it all. I could not tell what was real and what was the crazed product of my fever.

Dr. Robbins, who would not be our doctor anymore after we left Brooklyn, came to the apartment. He had to maneuver his bulk around stacked cartons in order to examine me.

"You have the Asian flooey," he announced.

To which I said, "Phooey," prompting him to award me a throat lozenge.

The next thing I remember is my mother saying, as we drove toward Long Island, "Of all the times you could get sick, you had to pick today."

I had never actually seen our new home. My parents had rented the upstairs half of a house on Coolidge Avenue, one long block from the ocean, and my mother described it alternately as a palace and a castle. She showed me a blurred photograph clipped from a realtor's ad.

So I did not know what to expect when we crossed a bridge onto a small island, Long Beach, but I remember hearing sea gulls bugling and thinking they must work for whoever owned the palace where we would be living.

Then we were all at the Beachburger, a luncheonette near our new place, and there was an enormous bowl of soup before me. I let a few drops trickle down my throat, then stared into the liquid, mesmerized by the yellow dots of fat, perceiving in the rice a pattern that dazzled my brain. It was a moment in which I had absolutely no sense of Home. I felt lost, as might be expected, without any image of my new life or the house in which it would happen. There was nothing to focus on. Beside me, my family ate in silence as I breathed in the soup's vapors. The only place I seemed to belong was in the land of sickness.

Looking back now, from the perspective of forty-six years, the boy gazing into his soup seems to be reading his future. It would not be an exaggeration to say that I was never entirely well again. A half year after recovering from the flu, I developed infectious mononucleosis. Common enough in people aged fifteen to seventeen or in young adults, a full-fledged, acute outbreak of mono is rare among American children as young as I was—barely eleven. Recurrences of mono are also rare, but I was diagnosed with the disease again in 1965 and 1967, signs of an ineffective immune system. From sixth grade on, I missed chunks of school because of various infections. Even in college, I spent feverish weeks in the infirmary on campus. After contracting the virus that targeted my brain in 1988, I heard my immune system described by an infectious disease specialist as "cascading," tumbling over itself in useless action triggered by the new virus while my body teemed with once-dormant viruses. My doctor said that I was both immune deficient and immune hyperactive, that my body's ability to recognize and fight pathogens was in a state of utter confusion. Over the last fifteen years, I developed a host of viral infections that I had escaped as a child, before my immune system went haywire: roseola, for instance, and even chicken pox at the age of fifty-five. 1957 still rules.

Sitting in the Beachburger feeling lost in time and space, I became convinced that I was an alien. After all, I was born on July 6, 1947, probably the single most famous day for UFO sightings in recent history. A wingless disc seen cavorting in the skies above California by an air force captain and his wife; an alien craft crash landing near Roswell, New Mexico, with a clap of desert thunder; a hovering oval spotted over the Kansas prairie; a glow above a Carolina bungalow: flying saucers were spotted in twenty-eight states on the day I was born. My mother often told me that I spoke strangely, squawking, singing gibberish, like someone from outer space. Maybe she was saying something true, rather than doing her usual berating as I supposed; maybe she was trying to tell me something significant about how I came into existence. Because, as I soon discovered, on October 15, 1957, while I was reading the secret message of my future hidden within the chicken-and-rice soup, a twenty-three-year-old Brazilian man named Antonio Villas Boas was abducted from his family farm by a crew of strange creatures who took him aboard their craft, which looked like a giant elongated egg. Later, after being examined by doctors and debriefed by experts, he was diagnosed with radiation poisoning. Though they had probably sickened me too, back when I was first delivered to earth, perhaps my alien relatives could not find me on October 15, since we were in the process of relocating, and had to settle for Antonio Villas Boas instead.

Over the next year, my family's new life came to look very much like its old life. My father got up early and drove to work in the city. While he may have loved his brother-in-law, he was utterly lost in the world of women's fashions, in the smell of leather scraps instead of chicken blood. My mother took a small role in a community theater production of *The King and I*, then stayed home and waited for the world to recognize her. My brother, succumbing to parental pressure, enrolled at New York University but did not attend classes, filling his days with drives back to our old Brooklyn neighborhood, games of touch football, and massive amounts of food.

Then we fell apart altogether. In 1958, my father was critically injured during the morning commute and would spend most of his next three years in hospitals before dying at the age of fifty-three. My mother learned to drive, bought a Plymouth Fury whose sheer size seemed to overwhelm her, and kept getting lost on the way to the hospital halfway between our new home and our old, unable to manage the world of schedules and directions and the unyielding facts of someone else's needs. How could she complain about her situation when her husband lay dangling from traction with both his legs shattered and his recovery uncertain? My brother, liberated from close scrutiny, quit school and went to work sweeping floors for our mother's uncle, who owned a children's dress business.

Later that year, I began taking evening walks on the beach near our house to watch lights winking at the horizon. Summer nights, I loved to float on my back in the ocean, which was eerily calm at that hour, and gaze at the sky, which managed to be both crowded and placid. Somewhere up there, in all that dark space, I thought I might locate my home. It took years for me to let go of the dream-like notion that I was secretly an alien and accept that I was, in fact, my parents' son. But I think I was correct in believing that I was sick all the time because my strange earthly world was unhealthy for me. My system could not adapt to the alien world it found there.

My mother no longer has a roommate. The gathering we saw last time in her room was a death vigil. Cleared out now, the room looks solemn. There is still a second bed against the wall, but its mauve blanket is tucked tight and her roommate's faded poster of a seascape that hung at its head is gone. The pearl-handled hair brush and dense lineup of family photographs are gone from atop her chest of drawers.

Only my mother's half of the room shows signs of life. But

they are minimal: three of her funhouse face drawings tacked onto the wall, a few empty lipstick containers on the credenza, strings of beaded necklaces she made at arts and crafts spread on a table top. To create room for them, her family photographs have been stashed in a drawer, as is her collection of my books. A still life in oil that Beverly painted for her hangs a little crookedly near the bathroom door.

In the solarium, my mother is staring at a fork. Having finished her soup and fish, she has pushed her lunch tray aside, placed a cup of rice pudding before her, and is trying to determine whether the implement in her hand is something she can use on the dessert.

"You can keep eating," Beverly says as we sit with her.

"I don't know how."

Beverly takes the fork and hands her a spoon. "It looks delicious."

My mother eats a little, then turns to me and says, "There's something I want to know."

I lean closer to her, but she does not say anything further. I take her hand. "What?"

She looks at her spoon for a moment. Then she shrugs and eats more pudding. Not only has she forgotten what she wanted to know, she has forgotten we are there.

"How do you feel, Mother?"

"I feel fine, dear."

"Do you like it here? Are you happy living in this home?"

She nods. "Except I don't have a boyfriend."

I laugh, which makes my mother look more closely at me. "Oh, I know you," she says. "I'm very glad you came to see me. You should bring your girlfriend next time."

I point to Beverly and say, "We got married, Mother. Ten years ago."

My mother looks at Beverly, then back at me. "I'm so glad. But where do you live?"

"In Amity. It's a long way."

"I know that song," she says, beaming. She tips her head

back and sings, "It's a hmm hmmm hm Tipperary." Singing continues to calm her as nothing else can, centering her in the place where lyric and melody come together, at home. Even if she does not know where she is, where we live, or how Tipperary might fit in.

"Long way to go," I sing back to her.

"Do I have money?" she asks. This question surprises me. Over the years since she has been in the nursing home, her range of questions has grown familiar—How old is she? Who was she married to? Does she have a boyfriend? Are Beverly and I married? Do we have children? Where do we live? This is the first time she has asked about money.

"Of course you do. And I take care of it for you."

She reaches into her pocket and pulls out a tissue. "I don't even have a penny."

"What do you need money for?"

She shrugs, having already forgotten whatever was on her mind. "To buy a home?" she asks. Then her eyes open wide and she laughs. "On the range!"

Wanting to steer the conversation away from homes, particularly homes out on the range like the one where Beverly and I live, I ask my mother how she feels. She lifts her hands to her face. Clearly, she is delighted to be singing; her face has lit up. *THIS is what I'm supposed to be doing!*

"I feel hmm hmmm, hm so pretty . . ."

To leave the Memory Impairment Unit, we press *1957* again. As I do, I think how appropriate it feels to enter and leave my mother's current domain by acknowledging that crucial and persistent year in our lives. I am also pleased by the sweet serendipity of this visit ending with my mother singing a tune from *West Side Story*, which opened on Broadway in September of 1957.

I believe that my mother remains happy there at the home. As happy as she is capable of being when she cannot even begin to make sense of her surroundings. People care for her, wait on her, ask her if there is anything she needs; there is singing from time to time, she likes the food, we visit her, and whatever may bother my mother at any particular moment is soon forgotten.

But I also believe that, until now when it no longer seems to register, my mother never felt that she belonged wherever she happened to be living. She could have lived anywhere—weather hardly mattered to my mother; neither did politics—and it would not have mattered. Home would always be some mystical place, an Upper East Side of Manhattan circa 1920 transported to, say, a fiefdom in medieval France. Where aristocrats were still aristocrats, cultural sophistication was whatever she herself said it was, and everyone could play the music to her favorite songs.

She remained in Long Beach from 1957 until Beverly and I moved her to Oregon in 2001. But in many respects, it never stopped being 1957 for my mother. That was the year she got her way, left Brooklyn behind with all the disappointments it represented, and saw her hopes dashed before the year was out.

I have long recognized in myself that feeling of estrangement from home. I may have inherited it from my mother, as I inherited her bulging forehead and serious nose, or I may have absorbed it from being around when her dissatisfaction reached its zenith. Even after no longer being convinced that I was an alien, I felt alienated from the places I lived. I left Long Beach in 1965, and went on to live in fifteen different houses or apartments or duplexes before settling in Amity with Beverly, in a small round house in the woods. I have been here for almost eleven years, by far the longest either of us has ever spent in one place, and have learned to be comfortable in the woods. But we are beginning to talk about moving.

In the car after leaving the nursing home, we sing a medley of songs from *West Side Story*. Beverly applies her graceful alto to "Something's Coming," that great paean to youthful expectation and high hope. I counter with a mostly on-key rendition of "Tonight," the kind of romantic love song that no longer feels silly now that Beverly is in my life. I know we are fortunate to have each other; that is, I believe, my mother's true message when she keeps asking whether we are married and where we live. As we slip into the early rush-hour traffic on I-5, we harmonize on "One Hand, One Heart," hoping to make it home before dark.

# 6 Billy Gardner's Groundout

The play was routine. A sharp grounder to the shortstop, who fielded the ball and threw to first for an easy out. It happened at Brooklyn's Ebbets Field on a Sunday afternoon late in the summer of 1955. The batter was a New York Giants utility infielder named Billy Gardner, the Dodgers shortstop was Pee Wee Reese and the first baseman that day was Jackie Robinson. There was nothing memorable about the play. But for the last forty-seven years I've never forgotten it.

I was eight years old, sitting with my father in box seats halfway between home plate and first base. He took me to several games every season, so this was neither my first nor last visit to Ebbets Field. It was just another game, with the familiar feel of being in the stands with my father on the only day of the week he didn't work at his poultry market.

As usual he ate peanuts and put emptied shells back into the bag they'd come from. He spent most of a half-inning struggling to open the top of a miniature bottle of Scotch he'd brought along in his jacket pocket. He rolled the program into the shape of a megaphone and razzed the nearby Giants' first baseman. He lit a cigar.

All of that is background to a perfectly meaningless play. When Billy Gardner hit the ball, I watched him run down the line and never looked away. Though the play wasn't close, he ran hard. He kept his head down, knowing there was little hope that he would be safe, and crossed first base well after the sound of the ball reaching Robinson's mitt. Then he slowed and turned back toward the dugout. I noticed Gardner's fair hair below the black Giants cap. I noticed that as he slowed his head bobbed up and down as though in full agreement with the umpire's call. He was out, all right. I watched his face—what I could see of it beneath the cap's bill—and detected no reaction to having grounded out. Then he simply trotted behind catcher Roy Campanella, who stood out in front of home plate as the Dodgers threw the ball around the infield. Gardner wore uniform number 15, and I kept watching as he entered the dugout, walked toward the end nearest home plate, and sat down.

There is no obvious reason why I should be able to recall this so clearly now, in the autumn of 2002, as I sit in my small round house in the middle of twenty acres of forest in rural western Oregon. But that moment has always been with me, recurring like a tune running through my head.

Forgetting is what makes memory work well. Our brains are set up to discard obsolete or unimportant information; otherwise, we'd quickly find ourselves overloaded with data. That's why we can't remember what we had for dinner last Monday, unless it made us sick or was unique in some way. We forget seldom-used phone numbers and the names of friends of friends to whom we were introduced at an airport six months ago. If the circumstances aren't special, we normally forget where we went on the morning of May 17 or what an acquaintance said to us on the street last year. Distracted by more vital matters, we sometimes forget that we have keys in our hand, or even why we went downstairs as we stand in the hallway and wonder what we're doing there.

If it is to be retained, information must be used, or must be embedded in memory through potent circumstances such as trauma, study, or vivid association. As Daniel L. Schacter explains it, in *The Seven Sins of Memory,* "emotionally charged incidents are better remembered than nonemotional events. The emotional boost begins at the moment a memory is born, when attention and elaboration strongly influence whether an experience will be subsequently remembered or forgotten."

The less we retrieve it, the less likely a name or phone number or event is to be kept in memory. Faces, the plots of old movies, the combination to a lock no longer in use—such detail fades into the mists beyond memory. We're better off this way, less cluttered, more prepared to keep and utilize what's vital. Or, as Schacter says, "a system that renders information less accessible over time is highly functional."

To persist in long-term memory, then, events must have real significance. Usually, that significance is negative. "The primary territory of persistence," Schacter says, is "disappointment, regret, failure, sadness, and trauma." Memories strongly linked with our emotional lives, what Schacter calls "hot memories," are the kind that typically endure despite our best efforts to forget them. This doesn't mean that positive memories can't endure as well—the first meeting with your wife, the trip to Ireland, the day you ran a marathon in less than three hours or saw a brilliant production of *Hamlet*. Only that tenacity of memory, which is made possible by chemical and biological responses to powerful experience, most commonly occurs when an experience is negative.

But what is strange is when an apparently meaningless event persists in memory. What is it about seeing Billy Gardner ground into a routine infield out that enabled it to remain with me as it has? Perhaps I've overlooked something. Blocked a traumatic or otherwise harrowing memory, or neglected something wonderful that is hiding behind the sight of Gardner's bobbing head, his number 15 disappearing into the dugout. "Persistence serves a healthy function," Schacter says. "Events that we need to confront come to mind" in ways that insist upon attention.

At this point in my life, I'm delighted when memories come to mind at all. Since 1988, it has become clear that significant parts of my autobiographical memories have disappeared or fragmented. I have learned to work with what remains, to seize upon whatever memories do surface, to ask questions and use research or music to help locate and connect other memories. I struggle to learn and retain new information. Yet that scene at Ebbets Field in 1955 has endured. The more I consider it, the more I wonder if that moment in my life was not as meaningless as I've always believed.

In her book *Context Is Everything: The Nature of Memory*, psychologist Susan Engel says "the process of remembering can only be understood as a kind of chemistry between inner processes and outer settings." To figure out why Billy Gardner's ground out has survived time and all the years of memories that competed for space in my memory, and brain damage and the normal losses of an aging brain, I should reconstruct the context. Sift through the facts, see what I can make of the chemistry at work between my brain and events that turned an unremarkable play into something I cannot forget.

It was September 18, 1955. It had to be, because that was the only game conforming to the conditions I set for Sean Holtz, Web master of the Baseball Almanac family of sites. I sent Sean an e-mail asking if he could find all games played on a Sunday at Ebbets Field between the Giants and Dodgers in 1954 or 1955 in which Billy Gardner batted and Willie Mays homered, something else I remembered of the day. Sean found two, both from 1955, and sent box scores.

The first game was played on April 24 and was an 11–10 slugfest that lasted four hours. I was confident that this couldn't be the game we attended because it was too full of drama; surely I'd have remembered something more from a game like that, won by a three-run homer in the tenth inning. Also, according to the box score's notes, the game's start was delayed twenty minutes by a downpour. My mother would never have allowed me to leave our Brooklyn apartment for a ball game under threatening skies, and my father would never have waited out a storm with me at the ballpark.

So it was the game of September 18, late in the season, and we were two among 13,491 people to watch the 7–5 Dodgers victory. Mays hit his home run in the sixth inning. Billy Gardner had two hits before being replaced by a pinch hitter, Dusty Rhodes, in the ninth inning. But it is one of Gardner's two outs that I remember.

It would be difficult to overstate my childhood devotion to baseball. I not only collected baseball cards, I read and memorized the information on their backs, kept them banded together by team, took them with me in an old cigar box on Sundays to visit my grandparents or cousins. Wherever I was, I played games of my own invention with the cards, spreading them on long hallway floors or on bedspreads smoothed to resemble the grass of a playing field, arranging them underneath dining tables, even inside empty bathtubs, devoting hours to these games and the compilation of imaginary statistics. I didn't just dream of being a major leaguer, I committed myself to the idea, and it wasn't until I was a nineteen-year-old freshman outfielder on my college team that I realized there was no future for a 5'4" erratic-fielding bespectacled kid with bursitis in his throwing shoulder who ran fast and had once hit a triple.

When I went to a game at Ebbets Field, I went to concentrate and learn. I went to prepare myself. To find models, so I could go home and practice my swing, practice my batting stance, tug my hat down on my head properly.

But why Billy Gardner? It would make more sense for me to remember vividly seeing Willie Mays, who was in his heyday in 1955. I believed Mays was the greatest player in the game. Despite being a Dodgers fan, loyal to our center fielder, Duke Snider; despite recognizing that the Yankees' center fielder, Mickey Mantle, was an astonishing combination of slugger and speedster; I accepted that Mays could do everything. And there I was, seeing "The Say Hey Kid" in person, seeing him hit his 48th home run of the season during that game. I vaguely recall the ball flying out of Ebbets Field, a lean and exuberant Mays rounding first base, the back and sleeves of his flannel uniform top flapping in the breeze as he eased into his home run trot. But it's mostly in shadow; I only see him in that one moment of loping between first and second base, and the image only comes back when I think about Billy Gardner and his insignificant out.

He was born William Frederick Gardner, in Waterford, Connecticut, on July 19, 1927. Though he was six feet tall and weighed 180 pounds, Gardner seemed slight on the field, a modest performer among players whose talent tended to dwarf his own. They called him "Shotgun," in honor of his strong throwing arm. They also called him "Whitey," after the fairness of his hair.

In 1955, when I saw him play, Gardner was in his second major league season. A typical good-fielding but light-hitting substitute infielder, he had appeared in 62 games for the Giants the year before, as an aging rookie who'd spent a decade working his way up through the minor leagues. He'd batted only .213 in his first major league season, with little power (one home run, seven runs batted in). He was versatile on defense, playing second base, shortstop, and third base, but 1954 had been an unimpressive debut season for Gardner on a team filled with impressive talent, including future Hall of Famers Mays, Monte Irvin, and Hoyt Wilhelm. All but one of the team's starters in Gardner's rookie season was named to an All-Star team at some point in his career, and his role as a rookie was a limited one. The Giants won the National League pennant in 1954 and swept the World Series from the Cleveland Indians, but Gardner didn't get to play in the Series.

Then in 1955, he appeared in even fewer games. Playing only 59 times, he batted .203, hitting a few more homers (3) and driving in a few more runs (17) while playing the same trio of positions.

There was little in his performance, status on the team, or prospects to have called my attention to Billy Gardner when I accompanied my father to Ebbets Field. Nor was his play memorable in subsequent seasons, so that I would have looked back to remember seeing a budding star. The Giants gave up on Gardner after 1955, selling him for $20,000 to the Baltimore Orioles at the start of the 1956 season and overhauling their entire infield. He played more frequently and slightly better in four seasons as the Orioles' regular second baseman, leading the American League in doubles in 1957 and establishing a record for his position with twelve put-outs in a sixteen-inning game. Then he drifted around the league for another four seasons, retiring in 1963 at the age of 36, going on to manage the Minnesota Twins and Kansas City Royals in the 1980s. Gardner's lifetime batting average was a meager .237; over a ten-year playing career he averaged only four home runs and 27 runs batted in.

It's as though I remember Gardner's groundout precisely because of his lack of memorability as a player or the absence of emotional display. The very ordinariness of the situation, the banality of the play, seems to be part of the point. What is distinct is the lack of distinction.

I remember being intrigued by marginal players, especially those on the Dodgers and their arch-rival Giants. Maybe this was an early sign of realism creeping into my career plans. I can more readily recall the names of Gardner and the other Giants' utility players from 1955—Joey Amalfitano, Foster Castleman, Bobby Hofman, Wayne Terwilliger—than the names of the starting players, the heroes of that team. The back-up players' images from baseball cards are clearer to me still, and their names are the first that come back when I think of the team. I identified strongly with these guys, perhaps more than with the stars, and I paid attention to them at the ballpark. It's like focusing on Angus McFadyen instead of Mel Gibson while watching *Braveheart*.

I believe I was acutely impressed by seeing Gardner cope with failure. This moment, with its drama built around public disappointment, seems to have been a moment of enormous emotional power for me, though not for Gardner. He knew he was out from the moment he hit the ball, but he ran hard and he returned to the dugout stoically, undemonstratively. And his failure didn't cause an eruption of criticism. The first-base coach didn't harass him; his teammate, Don Mueller, who was walking toward home plate to bat next, didn't frown at him; manager Leo Durocher left him alone in the dugout. By the age of eight, I'd already been trained by my parents to believe that nonperformance and defeat bore serious, often violent consequences. As in many homes of second-generation immigrant families in the 1950s, expectations for the children were high and tolerance was low. Nothing made me more anxious than having committed a mistake in front of them—spilling milk, leaving fingerprints on the wall, neglecting to put a toy back in its place, saying the wrong thing, displeasing a teacher—because such disappointment triggered immediate physical fury. It must have been bracing for me to see a major league player controlling his emotions when faced with failure, and authority figures who didn't berate him for it. To recognize failure as something that needed to be accepted with grace.

From a neurological standpoint, the persistence of this memory is explicable if I'm right in discovering such a hidden source of emotional power: I was deeply moved to see someone, only marginally capable of playing for the 1955 Giants, fail before my eyes and yet deal with the consequences as though it were not a catastrophe. In addition, since my goals in life at that time centered around being a ballplayer, and since I worried about being too small to fulfill my goal, seeing a player like Gardner ground out carried extra emotional significance. As Daniel Schacter explains it, "when we relate a current experience to short- or long-term goals, we engage in a kind of reflection and analysis—elaborative encoding—that promotes subsequent memory for the experience." It's true that I witnessed more than fifty outs during that Sunday ball game, but only Gardner's stuck with me. Maybe it came at a crucial moment in the action, or at the beginning of the game, since he was the visiting team's leadoff batter and would have been the first player to hit on that day. I can't reconstruct the exact moment from a box score. But I know that the moment has lasted for me, intact and intense, filled with emotion and meaning.

From a psychological standpoint, the persistence of this

memory can have other implications. Freud, for instance, was very interested in childhood memories, especially the negligible ones. In *The Psychopathology of Everyday Life*, he devotes a full chapter to them, having noticed "the striking fact that a person's earliest childhood memories seem frequently to have preserved what is indifferent and unimportant." That certainly fits with my Billy Gardner moment.

Freud acknowledges that there is a "difference between what attracts the interest of a child and of an adult." This makes me wonder at the innocence, gravity, and solemnity of an eight-year-old boy's fascination with Gardner's failure rather than Mays' success—my focus indicating either remarkable empathy or remarkable anxiety. I don't even recall the home run hit that day by one of my favorite Dodgers, Carl Furillo, whose nickname was Skoonj, which sounded enough like my family's name to make him a relative.

Freud also finds, in regard to these mundane memories, that "an unsuspected wealth of meaning lies concealed behind their apparent innocence." He is particularly intrigued by a phenomenon he calls screen memories. These are insignificant childhood memories which, in classic Freudian terms, "owe their existence to a process of displacement: they are substitutes, in mnemic reproduction, for other impressions which are really significant." In other words, by retaining the memory of Billy Gardner's groundout, I may be using a trivial recollection to conceal something that really matters, to resist the confrontation with other "significant impressions."

After years of analytical experience, Freud came to believe that "the indifferent memories owe their preservation not to their own content but to an associative relation between their content and another which is repressed." I don't feel the need to undergo analysis in order to liberate myself from Billy Gardner, but I am curious about what might be hiding behind him, if indeed this is a screen memory. I've already confessed to associating marginal players like Gardner with my fear of failure and my anxiety about not being good enough to fulfill my ambitions as a major league player. But maybe something else is going on. Was it seeing my father labor over his miniature bottle of booze? He wasn't an alcoholic, and I had no fear of his response to a drink. But his powerful hands—scarred and bent from years of working as a chicken butcher—seemed stymied by the task. Maybe that's what I was noticing, that he was failing. Failing to open the bottle, failing physically as he aged (he was forty-seven in 1955), revealing a previously unnoticed vulnerability. Or was it seeing him neatly manage the mess of eating peanuts and knowing that I always got in trouble over crumbs and spills? Hearing him holler at the Giants' first baseman, Gail Harris, and call him a bum, because I feared my father's raised voice? Oh God, there's also the cigar to consider.

None of that sounds completely convincing to me. But it's possible that, taken together, they add up to a fraught moment in my childhood perceptions. A flashbulb memory of a single event, laden with associations, in which an anxious, dreamy young boy who fantasized a doubtful future for himself as a ballplayer, got to spend a September afternoon at Ebbets Field with his father and noticed, simultaneously, a host of his father's significant gestures alongside a marginal player's failure. And never forgot.

I can't help wondering if something else might have been happening on September 18, 1955, something that could have upset me enough to require repression. Well, according to Google.com, it was the day that the United States issued a Fort Ticonderoga three-cent stamp, but I don't think this was a problem for me. Nor was the announcement by the British Foreign Office that, four years earlier, a pair of their diplomats—Guy Burgess and Donald Maclean—had defected to the Soviet Union, confirming the story of a former KGB spy. It had been a week in which Mitch Miller's "Yellow Rose of Texas" was the Number One song on Billboard's Top 40, just ahead of Pat Boone's "Ain't That a Shame," a season in which *The Lawrence Welk Show* debuted on television and *Oklahoma* was in the movie theaters and kids were wearing coonskin hats in honor of Davy Crockett.

It was, in short, a relatively mild time in the outside world that I knew. But as with most eight-year-olds, the outside world was far less vital to me than the inside world. I know that in 1955, my parents were approaching the climax of their lives in Brooklyn. Always volatile together, as they neared fifty my parents saw their familiar world crumbling and had few resources between them to maintain stability. My father's business was failing and, though unprepared for any other kind of work, he would have to sell his market, and we would have to move. It was all they talked about, thought about, argued about. I wasn't sure what moving meant; it seemed to me that people who "moved" were like people who died, simply vanishing from our lives. My parents barked, *Don't worry* when I asked for clarification, which made me worry more. And even the Dodgers were rumored to be leaving Brooklyn. Everything around me was threatening to change. And at a baseball game, amidst blossoming uncertainty, I failed to register the excitement of an action-filled 7–5 contest filled with star players and noteworthy performances, and focused instead on the calm, steady, reliable failure of a little-known infielder to reach first base while, out of the corner of my eye, keeping tabs on my suddenly vulnerable father's activities.

For fifteen years, I've been obsessed with piecing back together my autobiographical narrative from fragments that survived the viral attack in 1988. My father died when I was fourteen and my mother's memory has been ransacked, so those who knew me most intimately as a child can't help reassemble the story. Photographs are a great resource; so are cousins and friends from the past. I use music, listening to songs from the fifties when I'm trying to recapture the feel of things; I watch period films, use the Internet, reference books to help stimulate and connect shards of memory. But it's a tricky business to sort out genuine personal memory from images that belong to other people's recollections or to the culture at large. What is truly mine?

Persistent memories are among the most reliable, etched as

they are into the brain's chemistry by the aroused conditions under which they were formed. So I have learned to treasure them, and treat the most persistent of my memories as gifts from the wreckage, or perhaps I should say clues to the great scavenger hunt that matters so profoundly to me.

We're always shaping the past as we age, and as we age we inevitably lose so much of our story. What I'm doing is hardly unique, though it may have a greater tinge of urgency because of my brain damage, and is put in perspective by my mother's deteriorating condition. At ninety-two, she now has nothing left of her autobiographical self except fragments, and even those are few and widely scattered. She is at the point now where she doesn't really know who I am. I say my name and she says, "Floyd? The butcher?" She knows fewer and fewer snatches of song lyrics and melodies, and almost all the rest is now a kind of dust.

At this moment in my life, I think that having Billy Gardner and his groundout clearly in memory is a kind of triumph. Still being able to form a convincing account of why it has endured feels like a real victory over the illness that threatened to eradicate the integrity of my self. A vital scene from my childhood has cohered around this indifferent memory. As Gardner himself made his way from the small failure of September 18, 1955, to a fair career playing the game of baseball and then managing at the major league level, I too have made my way from childhood and from brain damage to a modest level of wholeness. I have memories, I have resources, and I have been putting my story back together again.

# 7  A World of Light

*They've all gone into a world of light.*

from "Grandparents," by Robert Lowell

It is Friday afternoon, so my mother is not in the Memory Impairment Unit when we arrive at her nursing home. She is in the front parlor, where a visiting pianist is entertaining residents. But Beverly and I have forgotten that. We have forgotten it is Friday, lost track of my mother's schedule, and are mystified when she is not at her customary table in the solarium. Has she wandered away, as we know that many Alzheimer's patients tend to do? We go back to check her room, then walk to the solarium again, as though it were possible for us to have overlooked her the first time.

We figure it out at the same time and come to a stop in the hallway. "Wait," I say, turning toward Beverly.

"Music hour," she says, turning toward me.

So we punch in the code and leave the Memory Impairment Unit, walk down the corridor, and hear my mother before we see her. The familiar smoky contralto is raised to top volume as it glides in and around the lyrics she has forgotten. And there she is, seated alongside the piano's frame, head back, eyes shut, belting out the tune: *hmmm where my heart hm hmm hmmm ever, down hmm hmm old folks hmmmm.* My first thought is that "The Old Folks at Home" is a peculiar choice of songs for a nursing home setting. Then I wonder how her fellow residents, sitting in chairs scattered around the room, feel about my mother stationing herself next to the pianist and accompanying her with a mix of remembered and fanciful lyrics, tuneful humming, and scat. But no one seems to mind. *All the hmm is hmmm and dreary hmmm hmm hm hmm hmmm,* she sings happily.

We move with her to a small table near the door. As she walks, she keeps looking wistfully back at the piano and opens her eyes wide to sing, *Everyhmmm I hmm.* Then she sits. "Tell me something, dear," my mother says. "Is that singing?"

"Beautiful singing," I say. "I'm impressed that you remember the words."

My mother nods. The pianist takes a brief break. In the silence, my mother continues to nod as she gazes beyond my right ear, beyond the old upright temporarily abandoned against the wall, beyond even the summer light shining through the windows.

"I remember," she says, continuing to stare into the distance. "Papa was a furrier. He and Mama had a shop near the Spanish Steps."

This statement, welling up from whatever darkened depths, is so shocking that for a moment I cannot speak. Beverly looks at me and I shake my head. For the last year, my mother has looked blankly at me when I asked if she recalled her parents and their fur shop, or her beloved brother's character, or any details of her Manhattan childhood. She seemed to lose her memories backwards, the recent past collapsing back down around her second marriage and then my adolescence and childhood and her first marriage like an imploded building. I had given up on hearing anything further about her life.

Now some random sparking of neurons has brought back the fact that Max was a furrier. But he did not have a shop near the Spanish Steps in Rome. Beginning with a small establishment in the Bronx and moving steadily downtown toward Manhattan's Upper West Side, Max had a series of shops in New York. However, for a year or so, 1965 to '66, my mother and her second husband ran a dress shop in Rome, selling fashions made by her brother in his factory there.

Conflating two clothing-related shops, bridging the half century between her parents' shop and her brother's, and the nearly forty years since returning from Rome, she has produced A Memory. And her memory triggers a glinting cascade of memories for me.

For the moment, all I can do is sing back to her about the whole creation, about roaming sadly. Which makes her cackle and raise her voice an entire octave: *still longing ba-da hm hmm hm-hm.*

Max studies the cards. His jaw juts and he begins to shift the pink plate of his false teeth, tonguing it out and in, mouth widening until his grin has flipped upside-down between the gums. He slams a deuce onto the table between us.

It is a Sunday night in 1954. I am seven, and getting to sleep over at my grandparents' minuscule Manhattan apartment for the first and only time in my life. My grandfather and I are playing a game of Casino while my grandmother washes the dinner dishes. Max and Rose live in The Bancroft, a building just off Central Park West on 72nd Street. Through their open window in the heart of the city I hear the sound of buses stopping and starting four floors below us. Horns honk. I am tempted to lay my cards face-down on the table and run to the apartment door so I can open it and turn the crank that makes the bell jangle. It is an old-fashioned, Old World noise, a grind rather than a tinkle, something only heard here, and I believe they have brought the bell over with them from Poland. It is as much the sound of urban life as those buses and cars. I cannot get enough of it.

Rose is in the tiny kitchen, barely large enough to contain her, which no one else is ever allowed to enter. I have stood outside its door and watched her pivot between sink and stove, wondering if she ever got stuck there and had to call Max to get her out.

The sound of her cleaning mingles with traffic sounds, with Max's moist mouth noise and the flicker of his finger moving along the fanned cards in his hand as he waits for my next move. Thick green drapes are pulled back from the windows but the apartment is dark, as it always is. The radiators occasionally click and hiss as though clearing their throats, just like my grandfather. Odors of black tea, flanken, and noodle kugel mingle with schnapps from the half-empty glass still on the table beside the cards.

Even at age seven I know my grandfather is losing this game on purpose. He throws down cards he should be holding, bypasses cards he should have captured, grimaces, shifts his weight on the dark-blue sofa. Mumbling deep in his throat, he emits a gargle of sounds like someone choking on stones. I believe he would make sense if his teeth were put in right.

"What did you say, Grandpa?"

He chews his teeth back into place. "Building eights, I said! Three plus five! See!" He leans over and points to each card, revealing to me the cards that remain in his other hand.

I think he knows I am holding an eight. When I use it to snatch up the build, he smacks his forehead. "Gevalt!"

My grandfather is the strangest person I know. At sixty-eight, he is older than any other man in my life. His hair is thin, wispy, and white where it flies across the dome of his forehead. His skin is deeply wrinkled, his brow gouged with furrows. He always wears wrinkled suits and stained, wrinkled ties, even at home, even after dinner. I wonder if he sleeps in them. He has an elephant's ears, a bulldog's jowls, a gargoyle's jutting jaw, and it sometimes frightens me when his roving eyes actually settle on mine. All his sentences end in exclamation points. Gruff speaking, he strings phrases of Polish and Yiddish around words in French to hold his broken English together, and I understand little of what he says. Unless he is watching television. Then, sitting on the sofa, he will turn his head toward the television for a moment, turn back toward the living room and repeat the last few words of whatever he has heard. "Police at the scene report that six people were injured," a news reporter will say, and Max will exclaim, "WERE INJURED!" Or a weatherman will say, "Tomorrow will be cloudy," to which Max will blurt out, "BE CLOUDY!" My favorite is when he is watching weekly variety shows: "We'll be right back, folks, so don't go away." "GO AWAY!" Which makes me laugh, which makes him frown, which lets me know he is pleased. I have come to believe that everything he says, and every gesture he makes, means exactly the opposite of what it seems. Like when he plays cards with me, where losing is really winning and a curse is a kiss.

Sometimes the things he says make me laugh when they are not supposed to. Between hands, I ask him where he went this afternoon.

"I took the boss!"

I thought he worked for himself, making fur hats whenever the mood struck him. "You took the boss?"

He nods. "The boss! Crosstown!"

"Why did you take him across town?"

"Take who?"

"The Boss."

"Because crosstown was too far to walk!"

At that point, my grandmother rescues me. "Max, don't tease him like that. He means the bus, Floit. The crosstown bus."

"That's what I said! The crosstown boss!" And he scowled at me as I laughed.

Max was born in Crackow, Poland. But when I ask him where he comes from, he lifts his head a little and says, "I'm a man from the world!" By which, I have come to believe, he meant *a man of the world*, but he seemed so otherworldly to me that I took what he said literally.

Max left Crackow when he was ten eleven twelve thirteen fourteen. He went to Paris. He went to England. Germany Russia Austria Italy. Sometimes he arrived in America younger than when he left Poland. "Already when I was fourteen I knew more English than you know!"

Names and specific places—facts—are elusive in my grand-parents' apartment. His name, for instance, is not really Max, but Markus. And Poland was sometimes Lithuania, sometimes Russia, a little bit Austria and Hungary and something called Prussia. Max has so many brothers and sisters that he cannot remember all their names, and waves them away when I inquire. "I come from nothing!" he says. "Nothing and nowhere! Deal the cards!"

Rose's name is not really Rose, but Rosa. Daughter of a tinsmith, she was born in Tuchow, a small town on the Biala River about forty-five miles southeast of Crackow. At the time she lived there, Tuchow was in a part of the Austro-Hungarian Empire known as Galicia, but now it was not. She came to America in 1901, with a half dozen sisters and a pair of brothers, but her family would only talk about four of the sisters and one of the brothers.

Though she is a year older than Max, Rose seems much younger. She is easily amused, and when she smiles, her eyes disappear and her face seems to be all nose, a great bulb jutting from the center of her open, rounded countenance. She is short, barely 4'10", and nearly as wide, as though having been compacted by work in that kitchen. In most of my memories, she wears elegant dresses, a double-stranded pearl necklace and a mink stole Max made for her. She carries a small leather purse so wrinkled I am sure it must have been a gift from Max.

He did not intend to marry Rose. But when he showed up at her parents' New York City home to court one of her younger sisters, Bella or Eva or Gladys, Max was told that he could see Rose or no one. They were married for seventy years.

When she is finally done with the dishes, I like to see them sitting together on the sofa. He makes a big production out of taking her hand in his free hand and placing them together on the fabric between them as though laying down the ten of diamonds, The Good Ten that is worth more points than any other card in Casino.

After finally managing to lose enough games, Max declares that it is time for an evening stroll. He puts on his gray overcoat with its fur collar, helps Rose into her full-length fur coat with the fox faces that dangle over her chest, lends me his massive fur hat which comes down to my eyebrows, and we descend in the slow cage of an elevator for a walk together toward Central Park.

This fabulous place where city and country meet is only

a half block away, but it takes us nearly a half hour to get there because Max and Rose stroll in the Old World style, promenading arm in arm so slowly that it hardly feels like movement. I start out beside Max, move around beside Rose, then realize that I belong behind them. My grandparents are a unit. This is their nightly constitutional, and my proper place is in their wake. But I am content to see them bobbing like a becalmed, two-hulled yacht in the evening breeze. Their heads lean together as Rose laughs in a way that makes her coat ripple as I watch. She has the happiest laugh I have ever heard. My favorite photograph of Rose and Max shows them standing in Venice's Piazza San Marco with fluttering pigeons on their hats and arms and all around their feet. They are laughing like children.

Being in their apartment without my parents present, walking near them, I am getting a glimpse of their truly private life. I do not know why this is the only time I will be alone with them. Perhaps I was too much of an intrusion into their cramped, perfect dwelling, their way of being together in old age, and my presence upset the balance of their living arrangement. Perhaps my parents did not trust them to take adequate care of me. Or perhaps I witnessed more than I should.

That night I discover that Max does not sleep in his suit. He also does not sleep in his bed. At least not for long. I wake before dawn, tiptoe through their bedroom to use the adjacent toilet and discover my grandfather sunk in the bathtub. His knees are bent to the right so that he fits snugly. The water is up to his nose and does not emit any steam. I do not know enough to check for ripples his breathing might create. Instead, certain he is dead, I tiptoe back out of the room and approach my grandmother where she lies on her back in their bed. She, too, looks dead; her mouth is open wide, her teeth are missing and her head is canted so that she seems to be looking at the center of the headboard. I reach out to touch her and she opens her eyes, which frightens me even more than seeing her as she was.

"What is it, Floit?" she whispers.

I point to the bathroom. "Grandpa."

She groans and says, "I know."

This sounds alarming. She knew, and she went back to sleep? "He's dead."

"No he's not. He's asleep." Then she raises her voice. "But if he doesn't get out from the water right now, I might go in there and kill him myself."

My mother is trying to figure out who lives where. Over and over, she asks if we have a home and whether it is far away.

"Pretty far," Beverly tells her. "We live in a small town called Amity."

"But who do you live with, dear?"

Beverly points to me. "With your son."

"You should get married."

"Floyd and I are married. For ten years now."

"Floyd? Oh, yes, Floyd Skloot." She taps her fingers on the table and repeats *Floyd Skloot* a couple of times. "I know that name."

"You were married to my father," I tell her. "Harry Skloot."

"I was?" She is agitated, squirming in her seat, beginning to look cross. But then, just above a whisper, she sings, "I'm just wild about Harry."

"You lived in Brooklyn, in an apartment on Lenox Road. Do you remember Brooklyn?"

"Is that where you live?"

"No, I live in the country. But Brooklyn is where I was born."

None of this is making her happy. The situation—my mother distracted and growing tense, me trying to come up with a way toward safer ground—is profoundly familiar. It makes me remember my childhood's alternate Sundays, when we prepared to visit my father's mother, Kate Skloot, instead of visiting Max and Rose. My mother hated those Skloot Sundays. When I was a boy, I would sometimes sing one of her favorite songs to defuse the tension as my parents got ready for the visit, hoping she would calm down, smile, lead me to the piano, and begin playing along. But it seldom worked, no matter how carefully I selected the song.

Now we are all ready for the piano player to return. When she does, and strikes a few chords, my mother relaxes. Her first song is "You Made Me Love You," that old Jolson blackface hit written by McCarthy and Monaco. Beverly and my mother lean their heads together, alto and contralto in sweet harmony despite the confusing turn the lyrics take. Feel bad? No: glad. No: mad.

But I do not join them. Instead, I am back in my grand-mother Kate Skloot's apartment, time-traveling while my wife and mother sing. It feels important, as I sit beside my mother and witness her decline, to salvage early memories. And the ones that need the most salvaging concern my grandparents, the generation that no one else in the family recalls, that will vanish into oblivion unless I can keep them in the world of light. Only the tiniest fragments remain, but when I raise them they turn bright as shards of mirror glass.

As a boy, I assumed Kate Skloot's permanently grim expression reflected her ongoing widowhood. My grandfather Philip had died in late winter, 1939, more than eight years before I was born, and everything about Kate suggested woe.

Our phone calls were haiku:

"Hello?" I would say.

There would be brief silence, then a long and desolate sigh: "Oyyyyyy."

"Mother, it's Grandma Kate."

I only knew my grandmother as a solo act, swathed in black with an occasional flourish of gray. She sometimes wore a veiled hat. She was five feet tall, thick and straight from fore-head to flat feet. Her drawn face was all chin, with lips and ears snugly fit to her skull. Her nose plunged as if to merge with her mouth. She wore bifocals with a small star on the temple piece; I thought of that star as Kate's jewelry. I do not remember ever seeing her smile. In the photograph I have of Kate standing in the same Piazza San Marco where Max and

Rose stood, she glowers at the only three pigeons with enough nerve to approach her.

Kate's Brooklyn Heights apartment wore the same grim expression that she wore. A narrow, tight line of hallway led past closed doors. Severe wallpaper covered with faded blooms seemed to draw off any light. It was even darker than Max and Rose's apartment, and felt more confined despite being larger. There were formal black-and-white family pictures on the wall outside her bedroom, arrayed like a genealogical tree that, no matter how upscale its present surroundings, was never really free of its New World roots in the Williamsburg ghetto.

Though I remember the apartment's physical appearance, I retain few memories of actual life inside. I never stayed overnight, never spent time there alone with my grandmother, have little sense of the person Kate Skloot might have been. The primary source of energy in her place, and the central family event of each year, was a Passover Seder held in my grandmother's living room. Her half-dozen children, their wives, and a dozen grandchildren all gathered around her table. Undecipherable prayers were chanted at breakneck speed, sweet wine was drunk, and then we all partook of the only meat I can recall my grandmother cooking: chicken boiled nearly to vaporization.

Her apartment gradually settled down over the following twelve months, and each subsequent visit felt more subdued than the last, the conversation more hushed, the mood more morose. As winter took hold, our Sundays with Kate seemed sunk in a silence and stillness broken only by the sound of a chicken boiling away on the stove.

Born to a family of bricklayers in 1886, Kate Tatarsky grew up in the city of Bialystok, an old textile center. Bialystok was part of Russia then, though now it is at the northeastern border where Poland and Lithuania meet. Emigrating to Brooklyn shortly before the turn of the century, the Tatarskys found their niche in the live poultry business. Kate married Philip Skloot at age seventeen; he was working in an undershirt factory, but the newlyweds were helped by Kate's family to open a live poultry business together and settled on Keap Street in Brooklyn's crowded Williamsburg neighborhood. They thrived, and the family—with its six children—moved to ritzy Eastern Parkway, at the northern edge of Prospect Park. The business was taken over by two of Kate and Philip's sons and divided into retail (my father) and wholesale (my uncle George) poultry operations. Kate retained ownership of the building that housed my father's retail market. As her son's landlord, long-widowed and living alone in Brooklyn Heights, she found herself in 1957 compelled to raise his rent, helping to put my father out of business.

I know from my aunts and uncles that Kate was respected for her business acumen and powerful will. As my grandfather Philip grew sicker from diabetes and circulatory problems, she held home and market together. But no one spoke of her personality, or of intimate moments with her. Kate Skloot was a force. Formidable, fierce in her sense that home and business mattered most, she was remembered by her children as someone who did what had to be done to keep things solvent.

Being a widow, it appears, was less problematic for her than being retired. She hated having nothing to do, and I imagine her sitting alone in her gloomy apartment, turned away from the neat arrangement of family photos, silent except for the occasional "Oyyyyyy."

There is a small gray scar on the right side of my head, in the space between my ear and beard. This came from falling onto a pencil point during a visit to Kate's apartment when I was three or four years old. I like to imagine myself lying on the floor, drawing house after house with trees around them and smiling extended families standing on the grass, then growing so bored that I fall asleep and end up on the point of my pencil. According to the story I was told, everyone was distraught because blood stained Kate's somber carpet and the white towel that was wrapped around my head.

"Where do you live?"
"In Amity, Mother. It's about an hour from here."

90    *A Pick to the Heart*

My mother nods. "How big a city is that?"

"Oh, it's a very small town. Maybe a thousand people live there."

"Did you bring them with you?" She looks around. The pianist is playing something by Debussy. "I don't know the words to that."

Even before her illness, my mother could not grasp the idea that we lived in such a small town. Not only a small town, but in the woods on a hill above the town. In a little round house far away from everything. *Can you get the Johnny Carson Show?* she would ask. *Who fixes the toilet?* It was as though I had forsaken everything that she and my father, and that both sets of grandparents, had worked to provide me. You have a pond with frogs in it? You drink water drawn from a well? *Why would you do that?*

Debussy segues into "Tradition," from Bock and Harnick's *Fiddler on the Roof,* and my mother turns toward the melody, her face softening. She begins moving her index finger, an orchestra conductor with a baton. Waiting for the right measure, she nods her head, then sings, *Dum dah de dum tum travel da da living, feed a da da dee dah . . .*

Why would I live in the country, indeed. Born in Brooklyn fifty-six years ago, I was a lifelong urban dweller until marrying Beverly and settling with her in Amity twelve years ago. The simple answer is that I would live in the country for love of my wife. I would also live there for the solitude and tranquility that is good for my health and my work. But the drift of this "conversation" with my mother and my memories of grandparents and the music of *Fiddler on the Roof* suggest another answer, something I have seldom considered. I would live in the country because it is in my blood. Before Brooklyn, a scant two generations before I was born, the Skloot family was a country family. It lived for at least a hundred years, maybe more, in the village of Volozhin, part of Russia's Jewish Pale of Settlement in what is now Belarus. Perhaps that is why I adjusted so readily to rural life, surprising both Beverly and myself, and why I am so reluctant for us to move away as we grow older. Perhaps what I have unwittingly done is reversed my grandfather's journey from country to city.

The one grandparent I never knew, the one most shrouded in darkness, is my father's father Philip. I have no pictures of him. I can remember nothing of his presence in family stories. But for years I have been trying to track him down, to imagine him as a real figure in my life. Researching family history, gathering information about Volozhin, I hoped to illuminate this most hidden part of my family's past. By doing so, I thought I might see if the journey that began for me in Brooklyn and brought me to Amity might be a circle.

Volozhin, a small river town near Minsk, was a classic eastern European Jewish *shtetl*. Jews arrived there in the middle of the sixteenth century. By 1766, there were 383 Jews in Volozhin. When Philip Skloot left for Brooklyn in 1892, at the age of twelve, there were 2,452 Jews in Volozhin. Poorer families lived at the base of a small hill; wealthier families lived on the hilltop, where the esteemed Volozhin Yeshiva was located. This archly conservative school of Jewish learning, founded by a student of the renowned Gaon of Wilna in 1803, is what set the town apart from most *shtetls*. It attracted students from throughout Europe, even from America, and eventually it attracted the attention of Czar Nicholas II because of its refusal to adapt to various decrees intended to secularize education there. The Yeshiva, made of wood, was burned by czarist troops in 1892. Shortly afterwards, four Skloot brothers left with their families, two settling in South Africa, where their name transformed into Sloot, and two settling in New York. My grandfather, who had been Yeshiva-bound, instead went to work in the Brooklyn undershirt factory where he remained until marrying my grandmother.

None of Philip Skloot's children settled outside New York City. Some of the next generation, my cousins and my brother, left New York but ended up in and around urban areas—Miami, Houston, Madison, San Jose, Mill Valley. Except me. For years, I have felt adrift from my family of origin, a fragment blown clear of their urban gravitational force. But perhaps a more accurate rendering of my journey is one of coming home rather than floating away.

"Home," as T. S. Eliot says in his poem "East Coker," "is where one starts from." The most mysterious quarter of my ancestry is the rural quarter, the Skloot family in their Russian village, where my name originates. That, I think, is where I start from, and where I have become comfortable. I never saw my grandfather, neither in the Old World nor the New, and that may be part of why I am so strongly drawn to life in the country. To find something of that missing quarter, to track my grandfather's spirit there, and make peace with the place I started from.

I know Amity is not really much like Volozhin. It lacks the hubbub and sense of community, the power to organize the lives of its people around dominant religious or secular leaders, the productive and self-sustaining relationship with its surrounding land. But for the last eleven years, living in Amity has brought me close to something vital in my soul, something I do not think I could have found by living in a city. A hillside forest to surround me, succor for my impulse to live more slowly and quietly as I move through my fifties. And life here feels bizarrely familiar, something I recognize as truly known to me, and comforting. In "East Coker," Eliot goes on to say that "as we grow older/The world becomes stranger, the pattern more complicated/Of dead and living." That, I believe, is what is happening in my life as my mother fades away before my eyes and I attend to a grandfather I never knew.

I am used to thinking of my grandparents, my father, and my brother as gone into pure darkness. Death, I feel, is a crossing into nothingness, and the only afterlife is in the realm of their survivors' memories. As my mother's memory vanished, and as her life force continues to dwindle, I think of her as moving into darkness as well, and taking whatever she knew about my ancestors with her. By remembering Max and Rose, Kate and Philip, I am not only spreading light into that darkness, I am participating in a process that Eliot describes as a kind of generational fueling, "a lifetime burning in every moment/And not the lifetime of one man only."

When we stand up to leave the nursing home, my mother begins to tremble. We have been preparing her for our departure, assuring her that we will come again soon, but the moment threatens to overwhelm her. She tries to stand. Then the piano player comes to our rescue, banging out the opening chords of another familiar melody from *Fiddler on the Roof.* My mother eases back into her seat. *To Life!*

# 8 A Pick to the Heart

In the summer of 1967, when I turned twenty, I became engaged to a girl who would not sleep with me, and went to work for her father, a landscape contractor named Giovanni Bruno. This was in Long Beach, New York, where the fictional Godfather Don Corleone had lived. The Bruno family's house was a seven-minute drive from the toll booth on the Meadowbrook Parkway at which Sonny Corleone was machine-gunned to death.

When Rosemarie Bruno told her father that we wanted to get married, the three of us were sitting in the dining room after Sunday dinner. Mr. Bruno stared at me for a long time. Then he stood up and looked at me for a while longer before walking away from the table. At the door to the kitchen, he turned back and crooked a finger at me.

"Come with me, College Boy."

I followed him into the kitchen, squeezing sideways past his wife, Angelina, who was doing the dishes and humming "Ciao, Ciao, Bambina" to the steamed-up window above the sink. He told her to go watch television in the den.

Giovanni Bruno was short, my height exactly, but his hands were massive. He leaned against the kitchen counter, wrapped his huge mitts around a half-empty mug and blew onto the coffee, though it had long gone cold. Without bothering to look in my direction any longer, he said seven words: "You hurt my Rosemarie, I'll kill you." After which he went out to the yard where his bulldozer was parked. I heard it roar at his touch.

I'd just finished my sophomore year at Franklin & Marshall College and had no idea what I wanted to do with my life. It had dawned on me that being a professional baseball player was unlikely, having injured my right shoulder during one truly mediocre season as freshman left fielder for a team that didn't win any games and attracted few fans, none of whom were major league scouts. I could also admit that going from intramural football and basketball to the pros in either sport seemed a little far-fetched as well.

As a teenager in Long Beach, I'd worked as a busboy, parking lot attendant, butcher's apprentice, day camp counselor, travel agency file clerk, and produce man in a grocery store. But I didn't see any of those as promising career paths. In two years of college, and based upon my performance in various required classes, I'd concluded that careers as an anthropologist, economist, historian, geologist, or logician weren't going to work out for me either. I did, however, find out that I liked to read novels, stories, plays, and poems, and write about them. In addition, I didn't want to be drafted and sent to Vietnam.

None of these discoveries particularly impressed Giovanni Bruno, who, when not referring to me as College Boy, called me *Jedrool,* which means "cucumber." What do you do when your fiancée's father calls you Cucumber?

I was fit and strong. But that didn't seem to count for much with him either, because I'd never done any work resembling what he did as a landscape contractor. Therefore, I'd never done anything he perceived to be of value. As part of the Bruno family business that summer, I would be expected to mow and edge lawns, trim shrubbery, lay sod, remove and replace concrete driveways and sidewalks, haul rubble in a dump truck to the county landfill, run a bulldozer, and do whatever Mr. Bruno or his son Joey told me to do.

I'd come home to spend the summer with Rosemarie, play two or three nights a week in a men's baseball league, and earn a couple month's worth of spending money by working for the Bruno family firm. Also to read, catch up on some of the classics I thought I should know, because I had to declare a major in the fall and wanted to be sure I made the right choice.

The first day I showed up to work for Giovanni Bruno, I had a copy of Dostoevsky's *Crime and Punishment* in the back seat of my car. Sure, it was a Russian novel, but I figured English majors needed to be familiar with it. I planned to read a chapter or two during my breaks on the job.

I went to high school with Rosemarie Bruno. We were in one or two classes together, but never dated, and knew each other just well enough to exchange generic inscriptions in our senior class yearbooks: *Dear Floyd: Best wishes for a successful future. It's been great knowing you. Good luck always. Rosemarie.*

Beneath her yearbook signature, Rosemarie's slender oval face gazed to the right, creased by the remote smile I would come to know well, lips flexed slightly inward as though about to ask *What?* Her chin and nose were sharp, as in a Modigliani portrait, and her dark hair rose in a firm flip at the jawline, with bangs like a row of commas across her forehead. She had been in the Homemaking Club, the Bowling Club, the Ski Club; she was a Red Cross Representative and a member of the Future Nurses Association. A good person, active, eager to serve her community, well-balanced. I remembered Rosemarie as quiet, shapely, and attractive in a self-contained way. She wasn't part of any clique.

In my yearbook picture, I looked like a fire hydrant. Short, squat, all shoulder and neck, I was on the football, baseball, and track teams. My commitment to public service had ended after a stint on the Freshman Council.

While I'd gone away to college in Pennsylvania, Rosemarie stayed home, living with her parents and attending Hofstra University. That's where she met my cousin Michael. They went out once, in late fall, and when I came home for the winter semester break, he suggested that I call her. We were eating our favorite lunch together, hot dogs slathered in coleslaw from the deli in Long Beach.

"You didn't like her enough, so I should call her?"

"It's not that," Michael said. "She remembers you."

"She probably remembers you now too."

I recall reaching over to catch a drip of slaw before it landed on his shirt, and I recall Michael nodding to acknowledge my rescue. He shrugged as he said, "Call her. She's nice. What, you've got somebody else lined up?"

*Nice* explained everything. Why he hadn't taken Rosemarie out a second time, why he thought she'd be more my type, and why I didn't have anybody else to call. Still a virgin at twenty, I imagined myself done with *nice* and ready for *wild*, for *savvy*. Where was all that free love I was hearing about? Besides, the last thing I wanted was a relationship that would reconnect me to the childhood scene I'd finally escaped.

On our first date we went sledding with a group of Rosemarie's college friends, all strangers to me. Sitting in the back seat with her as we drove toward her home, I was happily shocked by her ardor when we kissed. This wasn't what I'd expected from the diffident girl in senior speech class, and I thought it boded well for the rest of my holiday. But the next day, when I phoned her, Rosemarie started crying. She was embarrassed, she felt guilty, she'd sinned, maybe we'd better not see each other again.

I was hooked.

The first morning I showed up for work, I didn't know whether to enter the house as Joey Bruno did, and have a cup of coffee with the family, or wait outside and chew on a toothpick like Elroy James did. It was cold for early June, with a brisk wind from the ocean and heavy moisture in the air. I decided to stay outside but stand close enough to the screen door so the Brunos could hear me talk.

"What's that on your feet?" Elroy asked.

"Sneakers."

"Mmm hmmm." He closed his eyes slowly and shook his head. I noticed that he wore boots. "Brung gloves?" A pair of gloves stuck out of his back pocket. He stuck his tongue out and used it to flip his toothpick over. "Hat?" He shrugged, adjusted his Yankees hat, and turned away to study cloud formations.

Elroy had his own vegetable nickname. The Brunos called him *Melanzana*, which means eggplant. I knew it was a reference to the color of Elroy's skin, a racial slur, and was still wondering about the precise connection between Jews and cucumbers. I started calling our dump truck the salad bin.

Giovanni Bruno marched outside, stormed past me, nodded at Elroy, got in his pickup, and drove off. Then Joey marched outside, flipped a set of keys to Elroy, got in his car, and drove off. *Nice to see you guys too.*

As I joined Elroy in the salad bin, I noticed Rosemarie standing in shadow by the kitchen door. As I think about it now, in many memories of that summer Rosemarie is in shadow, even when we are alone together, kissing, embracing. That may be due to a trick of time, the peculiar light of memory. Or it may be a reflection of deep truth: the fading of her feelings for me, the absence of energy between us, my failure of vision.

The summer job with her family had been Rosemarie's idea and I'd accepted without giving much thought to specifics. So I hadn't ever mowed a lawn, big deal, how hard could that be? Swing a pick? I was sure I could do that. Drive the truck? Why not, I'd once used a standard transmission while driving my aunt's Volkswagen.

As Elroy backed out of the driveway, I tried to remember why I'd thought it made sense to work for the Brunos. Truth is, I realized, I hadn't thought anything. Rosemarie and I had been making out in her basement while The Lettermen sang in the background. She stopped me, said it would be so wonderful if I could be around the house all summer, and didn't I agree that spending time with her father and brother would be important to our future? I agreed, as I would have agreed with anything she said at that point.

Now I lifted my hand to wave at her just as Rosemarie turned away. I continued raising my hand to adjust my glasses.

And that was the high point of my initial day with Bruno & Son. I managed to mow a couple of lawns well enough on the straightaways, but had some trouble with the turns, gouging the grassy edges here and there, leaving a few tufts like cowlicks around trees. I had no trouble dumping grass clippings into the wheelbarrow, or pushing the wheelbarrow to the truck, but running it up the two planks into the truck's bed was a serious challenge. The first times I tried, charging up the planks like a gymnast approaching the vaulting horse, my wheelbarrow got away from me and I dumped the load of grass onto the sidewalk. Elroy got a big kick out of that.

As the day progressed, my hands blistered and bled, I cut myself with a pruner, and was, apparently, the worst breaker-and-remover of old concrete that the Brunos had ever seen. I felt myself growing weaker and hotter, drying out, becoming dizzy. As the day's final job drew to an end, with Mr. Bruno on his knees working with the newly poured concrete, I knew I was running a fever. As I walked past him toward the dump truck, I lost my balance and stepped squarely into the wet concrete he'd just finished smoothing.

I remember him looking up at me, shielding his eyes from the setting sun, turning to find Joey's eyes, and shaking his head. *Jedrool.*

It was the summer of "Light My Fire" and "A Whiter Shade of Pale," of "All You Need Is Love," "Windy," and "Ode to Billie Joe." As an aspiring English major, I could have done a better job understanding the lyrics of those hits and thinking about what they might mean. 1967 might have been the Summer of Love, but the hottest songs in June, July, and August, showed how confused and fraught love still could be.

In the awful poetry of Procol Harum's enduring song, there's the deathly whiteness of the woman's face, spectral to begin with and growing even paler during the song's progress, as though drained of life by the fandango and cartwheels the lovers are turning. The loveblind singer realizes that he's been missing what's happening in his romance, noticing little despite having his eyes open. Sounds alarming to me. The guy wasn't seeing what he needed to see. Then it was too late and he was surrounded by signs of death.

Then there was Windy, whose sudden transformation from calm to stormy was something I was all too familiar with in my own relationship. So was the sense of a loved one always poised to withdraw, to vanish beyond the clouds. I could never listen to The Association's hit without feeling a bit uncomfortable, though I didn't bother to figure out why.

The couple in "Light My Fire" faces the prospect of their love burning them up. Though I was all for fiery passion, and hoped we might eventually move beyond smoldering, I didn't necessarily seek immolation. And we all could guess what made Billie Joe MacAllister jump off the Tallahatchie Bridge, even if we weren't sure what he and the song's singer had been throwing off it when Brother Taylor spotted them.

"All You Need Is Love" sounded like an anthem for an era of love. Love itself was sufficient, The Beatles chanted over and over in their familiar-but-soon-to-vanish harmony. Theirs was a mantra that began losing its meaning in the repetition, a chorus sounding like the group's effort to convince itself of something it may not have been sure of. After all, the lyrics were pretty grim: no surprises left, nothing original is possible, everything's been done and everything's known. If you can't do anything new, if it's all a great yawning bore, then you might as well lose yourself in mystical notions of love. Then the song ended in a confused muddle of riffs and references to older music — trumpets playing Bach, saxes playing Glenn Miller's "In the Mood," a snippet of "Greensleeves," The Beatles echoing their own early silliness in "She Loves You." The song collapsed into noise, underscoring the point about no originality being possible anymore as it resorted to musical echoes, making sure we understood that people have been saying the same thing about love for ages now, and just look at the state of the world.

Hell, even The Lettermen, whose sappy ballads so often accompanied the basement make-out sessions that never quite got me where I'd hoped to go, were desperate in their love songs. They covered a vast array of sad old tunes in which they begged a girl who was obviously departing to pivot and take another peek at them before disappearing, urged another lost girl to come back to them, or confessed to going out of their heads over yet another girl. I should have known it was a bad sign that I was listening to their songs.

By mid-summer, Rosemarie and I had been engaged for about six months. We were planning a wedding in June of the following year, 1968. Exact details of whether a priest or rabbi would officiate, or if we could even find ones to officiate, or what we would do for money after we got married, were still unsettled, but we did have a hall reserved for our reception. When we first talked to her father about that, he'd immediately left the room.

"He's happy," Rosemarie said. "He'll be back."

Mr. Bruno returned in a couple of minutes, fortified with a jam jar full of red wine, and sat down. He didn't offer wine to either of us, and for a while all he did was nod his head vigorously. I wondered who he was agreeing with inside that fierce and troubled-looking head. He did not look happy to me.

"You know how much it costs?"

We did, having prepared ourselves for this question. I told him the amount, adding "and they want a $500 deposit."

"Something happens," he said, "I come to you for the money back, right?"

While I agreed, the lyrics of that winter's strangest new song kept running through my mind. Something was happening here, all right, but what it was had not yet come clear.

During the work week, we all returned to the Bruno home for lunch. Elroy stayed outside, eating his meal in the salad bin and then going to sleep. But I was expected to join the family inside and share the same spread every day, served from communal plates: dandelion salad drenched in an oily dressing; cherry tomatoes; crusty, fresh Italian bread; chunks of Parmesan cheese. Mr. Bruno drank his jam jar of red wine. Joey drank three Cokes. I drank endless glasses of ice water. Mrs. Bruno served us. Rosemarie never appeared, though I knew she was somewhere in the house, and I was beginning to wonder if my fiancée cared very much about spending time with me. After lunch, as father and son departed for the next job site, I would wake Elroy and follow the Brunos. This was always my time to drive the truck, since Elroy maintained that he needed exactly seventeen minutes in which to let his noontime dreams come to rest.

If we weren't doing an all-day concrete job, most afternoons were devoted to landscape maintenance. And Wednesdays seemed to be the Mafia days, when we took care of properties famous around town for being owned by mobsters. Because my lawn work remained iffy, and I still occasionally gouged a lawn's edge or sacrificed a seedling, and because Mafiosi were famous for loving their landscapes, Wednesdays made me so tense I couldn't eat my lunch. This never failed to amuse the Brunos.

"What's the matter, College Boy, you don't feel good today?" On the rare occasions when Giovanni Bruno smiled, his face fell apart. A network of fine wrinkles flashed across his cheeks and around his eyes like the crazing of glass, those eyes vanished into folds of loose skin, his chin fluttered, his lips vanished. If he actually laughed, his entire taut body shuddered for a moment the way I'd seen it shutter while holding a jackhammer. Then he grew very still.

"He looks pale," Joey said.

"A peeled cucumber."

"Limp."

"Hey, maybe he wants a glass of what-do-they-drink? Seltzer?"

"Ha ha ha. Alka Seltzer!"

*Fagiolini! Carciofi!* I thought to myself. I'd bought myself an Italian dictionary one evening after work, and by late June would entertain myself by making up vegetable nicknames for my employers. Green bean! Artichoke! As they carried on

about my lack of Wednesday appetite, I called them *Finocchio!*
*Asparagi!*

Over lunch on a Wednesday in July, I had a revelation. They
aren't just teasing me, they hate me. They think I'm absolutely
wrong for their Rosemarie, they don't want me to become
part of their family, they despise working with me, they are of-
fended by everything I am. This hazing wasn't some version of
an initiation routine, it was harassment and it was malevolent.
They wanted me to fail, to quit—the job, the courtship, the
town—and never come back. Not only that, Rosemarie either
knew this and was going along with it, or didn't know it and
was even more disconnected than I'd imagined. While she was
struggling to save herself for our wedding night, protecting
her virtue from my basement assaults, and smiling at me in her
distant way, Rosemarie's menfolk were struggling to be sure
there was no wedding night, and I was putting myself through
the double ordeal of trying to fight the whole Bruno clan.

What was it, I remember wondering, that compelled me
to carry on here? Either I was blinded by love or a glutton
for punishment. Already, I could sense that it wasn't love that
distorted my vision, because I was glad to find more and more
reasons not to spend my evenings with Rosemarie. Too tired.
Ball game. Practice for next ball game. Need to read. Have to
meet my cousin for dinner or visit my grandmother in Manhattan for her birthday or spend the evening with my mother
and her new husband.

No, I believe I knew by mid-summer that this was no longer
about love. So that meant there was something about me that
needed the sort of treatment I was getting from the Brunos.
If I'd wanted more of that, I could have stayed home with my
violent and unstable mother instead of going away to college.

It was also not about fun, or pleasure, or the satisfaction of
doing things well. At least I was saving my wages, since Rosemarie and I weren't doing anything to spend them.

My concentration was in shambles. Though it didn't seem
possible, I began making even more mistakes at work, and

couldn't blame them on fever and the flu. I pulled buds and young blossoms instead of weeds from flower beds. My mowing left lawns looking like crop circles, etched with secret symbols, instead of the neat grids our customers were paying for. My hedges were so uneven that Mr. Bruno usually had to finish the job, leaving the surviving hedges several inches shorter and thinner than desired. I took too long to break up driveways with my pick, and twice removed the wrong segment of sidewalk. I could not get the hang of turning the bulldozer. The only task I performed well was driving the dump truck to the county landfill by myself, with no Bruno along to witness the achievement.

Though I'd always played center field in the past, that summer I was trying to transform myself into a slick-fielding third baseman. Through June and July, my defense was adequate, but by August I'd started making errors, dropping grounders, throwing the ball into the dugout. I'd stopped hitting well, too, and stopped chattering with my teammates, no longer backed up plays in the field. As never before, I felt out of position and out of place on the ball field, just as I was with Bruno & Son.

I was only on page 202 of *Crime and Punishment.* I was losing weight. I was losing hats and T-shirts and work gloves that I'd taken off at job sites. I was, it is clear, losing my way.

On one of the rare evenings when I returned to the Bruno household, after showering and eating a solo dinner, I found the family gathered in the living room with a young couple I didn't know. The man wore a black suit, white shirt, thin black tie, and the pale skin of his ankles was visible above sagging black socks. The woman wore a long black skirt, white blouse, and black cardigan, with no skin visible below the neck.

No one spoke as Rosemarie led me into the room. They all watched without expression while I settled beside her. Rosemarie refused to look at me or hold my hand. Instead, she picked up her copy of a thin, newsprint magazine and began to study it. *The Watchtower.*

The visitor said, "Matthew, Chapter 24, Verse 6: 'And ye shall hear of wars and rumors of wars: see that ye be not troubled for all these things must come to pass, but the end is not yet.' You see? There's no doubt we're in the time of the end. It's on your television every night. So now accepting the good news is an urgent thing."

"A hundred and forty-four thousand," Angelina Bruno said. Her brow was furrowed in the way it furrowed whenever she saw me follow Rosemarie down the basement stairs. "I never knew that."

"This is why we're here, ma'am. Now look at Verse 14: 'And this gospel of the kingdom shall be preached in all the world for a witness unto all nations; and then shall the end come.'"

The Brunos all nodded at their guests. They set aside their copies of the magazine and opened Bibles instead. I felt a trickle of sweat along my neck triggered, I supposed, by the August heat. I kept thinking about taking another shower. Then about the next night's baseball game, which would begin our first round of playoffs, and what I was doing wrong on the field. I found myself remembering what my grandmother had said last month, after I confessed my unhappiness with the summer's work. *Think*, she had repeated. *This girl's family will be your family.* She was being so circumspect, never mentioning the fact that my fiancée wasn't Jewish. And I remembered the way Rosemarie had looked at me a few weeks earlier—as though she were seeing beneath the familiar lines of my face—as we leafed through my Bar Mitzvah photo album, which she had asked to see.

"'It is only the people that God approves of who will receive everlasting life,'" the visitor said. "Look here: 'My sheep hear my voice, and I know them, and they follow me, And I give unto them eternal life; and they shall never perish, neither shall any man pluck them out of my hand.' I ask you, could anything be clearer?"

As the talk went on around me, I recalled the scene in *Crime and Punishment* where Raskolnikov goes to see Sonia, the prostitute daughter of his late friend, Marmeladov, and they read the Bible together. It's the moment that begins Raskolnikov's final downward slide, whose end was already in plain view as I read. True, I hadn't killed anybody, and I wasn't experiencing Dostoevsky-level torment, but I was beginning to feel troubled enough to identify with Raskolnikov. This evening, with Rosemarie reading her Bible along with the Jehovah's Witnesses who had come to the Brunos' door, was helping to crystallize that feeling. Whatever was happening between us, it wasn't about drawing closer together as our marriage approached.

I hadn't been sleeping well. As the discussion progressed, I began to drift off. Whenever my head sank toward my chest, I'd start awake again, blinking, to find Mr. Bruno's narrowed gaze fixed on me.

A few mornings later, Elroy and I were replacing a length of cracked driveway in Lido Beach. He started at the top, near the garage, and I started down near the street. We broke up sections of the old concrete with heavy picks, then loaded the rubble onto wheelbarrows and ran them up onto the dump truck's bed.

Near lunch time, tired, distracted, I lurched after bringing the pick down hard and struggled for balance as I pulled back on the handle. The pick came flying out of the rubble and its point struck against my breastbone, knocking me flat.

As I looked up at the noon sun, I understood that I couldn't breathe, and couldn't call out to Elroy. But he'd heard the pick clatter to the ground as I fell, and heard the sound I'd made as I landed. I was bleeding from the chest, right beside the heart, and the area was already discoloring. Elroy thought I was dying.

He ran to the truck, then turned and ran back to me as though trying to be sure he hadn't hallucinated the whole thing because of sunstroke. He knelt down and, for the first time all summer, laid a hand on me. Gently touching my shoulder, he said, "I never seen nobody do that before."

A few moments later, Joey Bruno drove up to inspect the driveway. Without getting out, he called to Elroy: "That's all you got done? What's the matter, the kid asleep?"

"Hurt himself."

I heard Joey sigh and drive away. I tried to sit up. The pain flaring from the center of my chest seemed too large for my torso, and I lay back against Elroy's knee. Then Mr. Bruno arrived. He opened his door but didn't get out of the pickup. He didn't speak, either, just looked at me and Elroy posed in the client's driveway like a sacrilegious pietà.

"Hurt himself," Elroy said.

"Tell him not to be late for lunch," Mr. Bruno said before slamming his door and driving off.

When I felt able to stand, I asked Elroy if he'd take me to my doctor's office. It was two blocks away, the doctor was a family friend, and I was sure he'd see me if he was there.

The upper portion of my sternum, a triangular slab called the manubrium, was fractured. Had the pick landed an inch higher, the doctor said, or about three inches lower, it almost surely would have killed me. Any harder and it might have killed me too, driving bone fragments into the heart itself. I was, he said, one lucky young man. I knew he was right.

My summer labors were over. So was my summer ball playing. I spent the next week at home, finishing *Crime and Punishment*, catching up on sleep, dreaming over and over of Giovanni Bruno, dressed in a last-of-the-Mohicans loin cloth, shooting arrows at my heart. Behind him, Rosemarie watched, lost in shadows.

When I told her that I wanted to break up, she nodded the way I'd seen her father nod when he received news he expected. This was no surprise to her, and it didn't seem to be much of a disappointment either. She went upstairs briefly and returned with a stack of my record albums. We hugged, she looked off to the right and smiled a little, and I drove home.

Before returning to Pennsylvania for the start of my junior year, there were two things I knew I wanted to do, and had to resist. First, I longed to buy a bushel of cucumbers, peel them, let them molder, and dump the lot onto the seat of Giovanni Bruno's bulldozer. Second, I wanted to ask Rosemarie to return my high school football jersey, which I'd given to her early in our time together, and which I badly wanted back. But not badly enough to talk to her again. Instead, I withdrew my entire summer's savings, $500, stuffed it in an envelope, and brought it with me to Rosemarie's house. When I handed it to him, Mr. Bruno shrugged as though to say *it was my money in the first place*, but he did shake my hand. He didn't have to kill me.

I wouldn't go so far as to say the Summer of Love taught me to understand who I was. More likely, it taught me who I wasn't. Or who I didn't want to be: that helplessly romantic fool unable to see what was clear to everyone else, even to the woman I imagined loving; that inept young man trying to succeed at what he didn't wish to do; the fellow who tolerated abuse.

In the months that followed my break-up with Rosemarie Bruno, I changed nearly everything about my life. I declared myself an English major and embraced the work that came with it, something I hadn't done as a student before. I auditioned for the college's Green Room Theater and landed the role of Pompey the Bawd in Shakespeare's *Measure for Measure.* I stopped playing intramural sports, moved out of the dormitory, and took an apartment with two other actors from the Green Room. I met a woman after one of the performances of *Measure for Measure* and by late spring we became lovers. I wrote my first poem. The wound above my heart healed, leaving only a deep dent in the bone.

## 9  The Simple Wisdom

*Oh, for the simple wisdom to learn from our experience!*

from "At the Head Table," by Thomas Kinsella

In late June of 1994, it was still cold at Glendalough. Beverly and I wore the winter jackets we'd almost left back home in Oregon, where it had been eighty-five degrees.

Glendalough, whose name means "the glen of the two lakes," was founded as a monastery in County Wicklow by St. Kevin in the year 498. Isolated and tranquil a millennium and a half ago, Glendalough now is crowded with tourists, even on a day like this. Low clouds heightened rather than obscured the lush green. We looked at the gateway arches and the cashel; at the ancient burial stones, some flat to the ground, others lined up against the wall like sentinels; at the great round tower that's supposed to be the best-preserved in all of Ireland. But my eyes kept returning to the man beside me, just turned sixty-six, his remaining hair and thick beard pure white, as he bent over the same tombs he must have shown hundreds of visitors by now but was still willing to show us.

I'd dreamed of visiting him for almost a quarter century. It had been that long since I last saw him, though we'd written and spoken often, always promising to get together.

As we'd left his house in nearby Laragh, Beverly snapped an unposed picture of him striding toward his wife and their Volvo, coat and umbrella gripped in one hand. I thought I saw it then, and when we got home and had the pictures developed it was the first thing I looked for: unbelievable. Beverly had captured something rarely seen in print. Thomas Kinsella was smiling.

In 1968, Kinsella was, according to the picture on his book's cover, a solemn, strictly formal man. Not exactly the image of a poet in those days of social upheaval. Wide-eyed behind Buddy Holly glasses, he looked as though smiling would be possible but not likely. Gray suit, white shirt, black tie. No beard, not much hair, no excess bulk. *Crisp* was the word that came to mind. Anti-hip. He looked, I thought, like a sonnet.

All of which seemed ideal to me because I knew poetry was Serious Business. I was twenty-one, a college senior who already had the answers to so many questions that there was little left to ask about. This attitude rendered decision-making easy, which was why I'd allocated a mere half-hour to selecting the graduate school I would attend.

Fatherless for one-third of my life, an urban Jew in the process of lapsing, I was, it seems to me from a distance of thirty-four years, looking for a structure, not a school. A purpose, too, because by then I'd had to accept that there would be no playing center field for the Dodgers, no playing Hamlet off-Broadway. Having written poetry for a year and read it for only a little longer than that, I knew that Poetry was what I wanted to do with my life. Besides, there was a draft to be avoided. Graduate school was clearly my most suitable option.

So I stood in the Franklin & Marshall College bookstore browsing poetry collections and anthologies. Late autumn, Richard Nixon newly elected, Jacqueline Kennedy newly remarried, students at San Francisco State newly on strike, Death newly defined by the American Medical Association: things were changing fast. I was ready to act on my new sense of vocation.

The first step, obviously, was finding the right university-based poet to study with. Once I found him, I would worry about such tangential issues as where the school might be located, what its admission requirements might be, whether I could afford it and what programs of study it offered. I began my graduate school investigations by perusing the poems of Auden, Bly, Creeley, moving through the shelves in alphabetical order, mentor-shopping.

I skipped poets whose work suggested they would not be right for me, whatever that meant. As I got to "K," I remembered one of my favorite poems, "Another September," by Thomas Kinsella. He was an Irish poet I'd found in an anthology where a hundred poets were each asked to select a favorite among their own works and comment upon it. I was drawn to the tightly rhymed poem with its modestly sexy domestic scene ("Stranded hair/Stirs in the still linen") rescuing a brooding loneliness ("Locked fast inside a dream with iron gates"). I also liked Kinsella's terse remarks in the section devoted to poet commentary: "Having remained inarticulate for most of my youth, I discovered more or less simultaneously the means of poetic expression and of honesty in love." Yes! Study with this man!

But there were no books by Kinsella in the store. Fate, I assumed, was against us, because it was Now or Never for me and Kinsella didn't have a book available. I planned to have my future settled by 3:15. Under "S" I found Anne Sexton, whose reading at Goucher College I'd just attended. Beautiful woman. She cried when she read those intimate poems that often rhymed. A very popular, very troubled soul. Yes! Study with this woman!

At the end of the shelf, where anthologies were kept, I found a new Oxford Paperback entitled, simply, *Poems*. It contained a sampling of work from Kinsella, Sexton, and the South African poet Douglas Livingstone. Fate was back at work: Kinsella and Sexton together must be a sign. Or maybe I should go to South Africa, if that's where Livingstone still lived, and study with him since a branch of the Skloot family had emigrated there in 1892. As good a reason as any.

Then I looked at Kinsella's face on the cover. I reread "Another September" and went through the other twenty-one poems in Kinsella's section of the book, becoming elated. His stuff was as solemn and strictly formal as he himself seemed; it had little humor or color, was winched to a taut elegance. There was the poem "Mirror in February," which struck me as overwhelming. The brooding poet stands before his shaving mirror "riveted by a dark exhausted eye,/A dry downturning mouth." Ah, exactly what I thought a poet should do and be. The more I read, the more Kinsella appealed to me. Poetry was, I believed, mostly about creating beautiful things out of a dark and gloomy knowingness. It was my proper calling and, I felt, the great tradition that Kinsella belonged to was strong enough to support me as well. Style was the man, I could see; everything consistent there, just the way I yearned to be.

Ireland. I should go to Ireland to study with him. This sounded both romantic and noble, the country of Yeats and the wee people where, at 5'4", I would feel right at home. This convinced me. But the biographical note said that he lived in America now.

Which explains why I moved to Carbondale, Illinois, the following summer. At no point did I even think to correspond with Kinsella. I didn't find out if he taught a poetry writing course or was willing to work with individual students, or with me in particular. Or if he was planning to remain at Southern Illinois University. I applied, was accepted and given a teaching assistantship, and spent most of the summer pointlessly sharpening my baseball skills in yet another men's league on Long Island.

Southern Illinois University is located in a part of the state known as Little Egypt. According to legend, the name had to do with the area's geology: a long valley seasonally flooded by the Mississippi, just as Egypt was enriched by the Nile. Or it had to do with great plagues that beset the region, famines and locusts and, again, floods. Or with an abundance of grain, as in biblical Egypt, and the long pilgrimages required of those who wished to buy it. There are towns in Little Egypt named Thebes, Karnak, Dongola, Joppa, and Cairo, which Illinoisans pronounce Kerro, and the university's mascot is an Egyptian canine, the saluki.

This was a long way from Brooklyn and the Jewish enclaves

of Long Island where I grew up. The landscape was not what I expected of Illinois, which was supposed to be flat, boring cornfields south of Chicago. I hadn't realized southern Illinois was where the glaciers stopped, that it was all cliffs and lakes and forested hills, parks with ominous names like Devil's Kitchen, Crab Orchard, the Trail of Tears Forest, or The Garden of the Gods. I might feel a little out of place, initially destabilized, but that would be good for a young poet. After all, what else were the late sixties for? All assumptions canceled. Yes, it might be good, provided the young poet had a mentor like the Kinsella I imagined, someone reliable and stable in his art, untouched by what was happening all around us.

I finally met him in September 1969. The only course he offered was a seminar in modern poetry. We were all seated around the table when he marched in and announced "I'm Kinsella," with the accent on KIN, not SELL. He didn't even know how to pronounce his name properly! He also wore a dark beard now, less insistent eyeglasses, and was larger than he'd looked in his picture. The voice was deeper and more resonant than I had anticipated. While he was neatly dressed and trimmed, there was also something loose and charged about him, something barely contained. Maybe this guy was an imposter.

Then he started talking about poetry. Handing out copies of D. H. Lawrence's "Autumn at Taos," a teeming excessive paean to a state of mind, Kinsella asked us what we thought of it:

Like yellow hair of a tigress brindled with pines.
Down on my hearth-rug of desert, sage of the mesa,
An ash-grey pelt
Of wolf all hairy and level, a wolf's wild pelt.

Well, I knew what I thought of it. The poem needed some work. First of all, it had to be tightened up. The feelings had to be brought under control, the menagerie thinned out, sentimentality eliminated with rigor. But I kept uncharacteristically quiet and listened as Kinsella read the thing aloud in his clipped voice, highlighting the repetitions and echoes, building a sense of urgency.

He seemed to love this poem, though nothing I knew about his work suggested that he should. He entered it fully, engaged with it, believed in it. "Under the pines/I go slowly/As under the hairy belly of a great black bear." More animals! More hair! What was going on here?

He acknowledged the poem's flaws and mannerisms, but said that "Autumn at Taos" was onto something he valued and wanted to do himself. It came so close to the thing it was perceiving. Kinsella talked about stripping away everything that stood between the song and its expression, things like predetermined forms and logic, imposed shape, literary reference, anything that implied the presence of a writer behind the poem.

Good lord, I was in Little Egypt for this? The Kinsella I'd come to study with wrote a poem about turning thirty-three, the age of Christ, that ended in a rhyming couplet: "I fold my towel with what grace I can,/Not young and not renewable, but man." The Kinsella I found was admiring "trot-trot to the mottled foot-hills, cedar mottled and piñon;/Did you ever see an otter?" He talked about an articulated descent into the psyche, admitted to toying around with automatic writing, wanted poems that dictated their own forms.

I didn't want surprises; I wanted order, certainty. I wanted rules.

Shortly after classes began, Kinsella reluctantly agreed to begin meeting privately, at his home, with three young poets who wouldn't otherwise stop bothering him. As I'd walked in the campus woods on the autumn afternoon following that first class, I realized that Kinsella might be undergoing a personal and artistic upheaval. After all, he'd moved from Ireland to Illinois, given up a safe bureaucratic career back home to teach in middle America, and seemed to be shifting away from everything that had defined his achievement as a poet. Like the leaves, which as a Brooklyn boy I had been used to ignoring, the man was changing his colors. Not dying, not drying up, but turning into something new. Okay, not like the leaves. But at least I was beginning to look outwards a little, using what I saw around me to make sense of what I felt. He'd already taught me something.

Kinsella kept surprising me. He came across as stable, organized, efficient. He did things with attention to detail and precision. His beard was so closely trimmed that some afternoons the tracks of electric clippers were still clearly visible under his chin. Nothing would escape his scrutiny. Before accepting the offer from Southern Illinois University, he had been an administrator in Ireland's finance department and seemed entirely capable of *management*. Externally, even down to the appearance of his classic suburban home in nearby Carterville, he seemed the essential conservative. He lived well outside the university town which, in 1969 and 1970, was in increasingly radical turmoil. By May of 1970, classes would be shut down and the National Guard imposing a curfew. Kinsella kept his distance. In an era of long hair and shaggy faces, bell bottom pants and Nehru jackets and Ben Franklin specs and open marriages, Kinsella at forty-one radiated traditional values. But in his work, he was ruthlessly overthrowing tradition and conformity.

"I want," he said to us one afternoon, "to stop from being crippled by form."

His poems were often formless, spontaneous, difficult to access. They followed the psyche's murky associations rather than the traditional flow of poetic logic. Kinsella called this work "automatic, subterranean" in contrast to his earlier "attempts to arrange rather than communicate." His poetry was ragged, wild, "a tangle of concerns," and he said it seemed to him "more relaxed, profound, interesting." It was for him "a new kind of writing that dictates its own form." I never knew what to expect from his poems now, though I grew fairly certain of what to expect from him.

Tuesday nights, Gerry Mills, Bob Randolph, and I would

drive the ten miles east to Kinsella's house and be led into one of two rooms. On rare occasions when he would discuss our own poems, we went into the living room; if we were discussing *real poems* like "Fern Hill" or "Marina" we went into the dining room to sit at a long rectangular table, huddled over our copies like gamblers lit by the low chandelier. There he admired poems I was sure he'd hate, like Robert Creeley's abstract "The Finger," and introduced me to the work of his fellow Irish poets James Clarence Mangan, Austin Clarke, Patrick Kavanagh, Richard Murphy, John Montague, Seamus Heaney. While I waited for us to do the important work—reading my poems, or maybe reading and discussing some of his—Kinsella was helping me read and appreciate the range of options I had as a writer. And he was offering me, in his dedication and openness and curiosity, a model for how a poet develops.

A poet, I discovered, hoards his privacy, can actually be reticent and self-contained about his work and life. A poet can be a dedicated husband and father. He writes all morning and does not come to the telephone when called during that time, does not schedule classes or meetings. He keeps the writing sacrosanct, and simply does it, every day. I never got to see his writing room, the notes and diagrams he once mentioned as being taped to its walls, the books he kept around the desk. I never saw him at work, not even making notes for his work.

I arrived at his house early one evening and was admitted with customary grace by his wife Eleanor. I loved Eleanor, drawn to her warmth and elegant beauty, her courage in dealing with the myasthenia gravis that weakened her. This particular night, she led me into the kitchen from which, in place of the typical quiet that distinguished the house, I heard a loud, steady pounding.

I remember that Kinsella wore an apron, though this could easily be a bogus detail, and that he was smiling when I came in. He held a mallet in his raised right hand. On the kitchen counter was a cutting board and on the cutting board a thick pink cow's tongue, which he resumed battering. His blows were measured and careful, but full of power and intensity. I didn't know what to watch, the tongue bouncing on its board, Kinsella's arm as it rose and fell, his face as it glowed with good humor. *The only. Way. To make it. Tender.* The scene was so rich with metaphoric possibilities that I could hardly control the urge to get out my notebook. Poet Subdues Tough Tongue!

For Christmas in 1969, his three poetry students brought a bottle of Jameson's Irish Whiskey. He took it from us at the door, read the label closely, turned to clear a place for it on a nearby credenza, smiled, and said, "We'll discuss this later." Then he led us to the dining room for our reading of Austin Clarke's poem "Ancient Lights."

That same Christmas, he came with Eleanor to a small party at Gerry Mills' house. When Kinsella entered the place, Gerry was still decorating the tree.

"What do you think?" Gerry asked, dangling one more ornament from his hand. "Where should this go?"

Kinsella paused for a second, then shook his head and said, "The thing's perfect as it is. Anything else would be strictly for effect."

He spoke with reserve, succinctly, and without blarney, which made his stealthy humor most effective. Slowly, my feeling of reverence was being transformed to delight. He could be a hoot, after all. I began to copy his style of banter. I grew a beard and kept it closely trimmed. I tried to write about Kinsellan dark caves, the drip of moisture from stalactites, the creepy feel of, I am ashamed to recall, "the stalagmites of nightmare."

The highlight of the year I spent in Kinsella's company was a conference sponsored by the American Committee for Irish Studies. It was held at Southern Illinois University in early 1970, bringing poets John Montague and the young Seamus Heaney to town for readings, as well as a number of scholars who would make presentations about their areas of specialization. The only scholar I recall meeting there was Professor John V. Kelleher, from Harvard, who was greeted with great enthusiasm by the poets. Kinsella later mentioned that Tim Pat Coogan was there, a former editor of the Irish Press and author of several books on the IRA and Irish history. He also mentioned a midnight swim in Crab Orchard Lake that I somehow missed.

What I remember is the gathering of poets. There was the official business of readings on campus—my first exposure to Heaney's earthy, mesmerizing voice and delivery and to Montague's way of reading across his stutter to heighten the emotional effects. Kinsella read from his new translation, *The Táin*, rather than from his new poetry. It was the first and only time I ever heard him present his work in public.

Then there was the private business. I had been assigned to transport Montague to and from campus, and to be certain he arrived for his reading on time and in good physical condition. Beyond those errands, most of the weekend was spent at Kinsella's home. One evening the poets and scholars sat in the family room and took turns singing traditional songs. Another evening, in the living room, Kinsella, Montague, and Heaney sat in a semi-circle discussing a new anthology of Irish poems in which, as I recall, the editor included as many of his own poems as those of Yeats.

Here, I thought, I was seeing the real thing. Poets at their hard-earned, alcohol-fueled play. The mutual respect among those three was evident, as well as a joy at being together in this foreign place. Though I didn't realize it at the time, I was also seeing the end of my mentorship. Kinsella left Southern Illinois University and Carbondale just a few months after this gathering. He accepted a position with Temple University in Philadelphia, which would allow him to spend half of each year back in Ireland, leading students on literary tours of the country.

When I heard he was leaving, I was stunned. It happened so fast, and with such little warning, that I felt abandoned, as I did after my father's sudden death in 1961. But soon I was considering options. Having nearly completed my MA, should I transfer to Temple next year for a PhD so I could keep working with Kinsella? Should I transfer elsewhere, to work with another poet? I went so far as to apply to a number of graduate programs with this in mind, eventually getting accepted at Louisiana State University, the State University of New York at Stony Brook, the University of Iowa Writer's Workshop, and Vanderbilt University. But by then, I'd realized that there was no need to study with anybody anymore.

I'd gone to Southern Illinois University with the cockamamie notion that Kinsella would teach me the secrets of successful poetry writing. Craft and technique, certainly, but something more as well—a way, perhaps, of selecting material, of thinking about the poem in order to fashion good work, of revising with a magic touch. Short of locking me out of his house, he could not have met this intention with greater resistance, and in time I began to understand why. Instead of teaching me how to write, he taught me a little about what a writer is, and what the writing life is about, with poetry at its center. Reading, writing, revising, arguing, mocking, reviewing—there was a wholeness to the life of a poet that I had never begun to consider, and it didn't matter what else a poet did.

In the summer of 1972, rather than dogging Kinsella's life any further or moving on to study with another poet, I accepted a job as a budget analyst with the Illinois Bureau of the Budget. I suppose that, like growing a beard, going to work as a bureaucrat in the state's finance department was a further effort on my part to Kinsellize myself. I may have gotten over my urge to study with a poet, but apparently it would still take some time for me to claim my own poetic life.

Nevertheless, I was on my way into the world, and into a process of discovering whether I would be able to center my life around poetry. The first thing that happened, and probably the best thing, is that I wrote nothing for over a year. I concentrated on my new job and its strange demands, started a family, read, exchanged letters with Kinsella. And one afternoon, early in 1974, I found myself writing a poem. It came urgently, clearly, and in a voice I recognized as something like my own.

I see now that my memories of Kinsella in 1969 and 1970 have little to do with the time I was actually with him. A few classes and evening meetings, a few isolated moments in his presence, some snatches of conversation. I remember reading his work much more clearly than I remember being with him. I had to get away, live my life, and work. Which was, of course, the message of his own life, work, and teaching.

The first letter I have from Kinsella is dated February 26, 1973, about eight months after I'd begun my new life as a budget analyst. In time, I began sending him my new poems which he would return with fewer and fewer comments. Finally, in April of 1976, he wrote a letter that seemed to liberate me. "My lack of detailed comment on your poems," he said, "is simply due to my recognition that you are out on your own." I construed this, perhaps wishfully, to mean that he felt I was writing fully as myself, and didn't need the sort of guidance I was seeking from him.

Our correspondence continued over the subsequent three decades, but we never managed to meet. Then in 1994, with Kinsella's support, I was granted a one-month residency at the Heinrich Böll Cottage on Achill Island, off the west coast of Ireland. I was forty-seven, considerably older than Kinsella was the last time I saw him.

I spotted Eleanor Kinsella as soon as Beverly and I passed through customs at Dublin Airport. When I'd known her, Eleanor had always been sick and virtually silenced by her illness, so seeing her radiant with good health and talkative seemed a miracle. She drove us past the city and into the Wicklow Mountains an hour south, where Kinsella would be waiting—and, I knew, working—at their home near Laragh.

Beverly and I slept for a few hours after lunch, then had a tour of the house. For the first time in my life, I entered Kinsella's work space. Over the next two days, we crisscrossed Wicklow, drove across the Sally Gap, went to Dublin to see where Kinsella had grown up, where he and Eleanor had met and lived, the streets and buildings he'd written about. We cooked them dinner one night, drove out to see a house where Synge had lived, another where Heaney had lived, a third where the Kinsellas' daughter lived.

Then Eleanor dropped us off at the train station in Dublin and we went for our month on Achill Island. At the end of our stay, we met the Kinsellas for dinner in Dublin. I gave him a notebook filled with the poems I'd written at the Böll Cottage; Beverly showed them some of the paintings she'd done. As we waited for our meals to arrive, the talk drifted across the last quarter century and settled on the topic of illness. Eleanor had fought back from myasthenia gravis; Kinsella himself was dealing with a painful skin condition and the aftereffects of problems caused by medication; and I had been sick, at that point, for six years. Only Beverly failed to contribute her share of woe.

"This," Kinsella finally said, "is like a scene from a Beckett play. Everyone takes turns chronicling ailments, and there's always one character sitting silent in the corner, just waiting for the right moment."

"Well," Beverly said. "I grew up wearing a full-body brace because of scoliosis."

At that, Kinsella threw back his head and laughed with delight. "There it is!" he said.

Outside the restaurant, we all hugged and I realized it was the first time I'd ever done that with Kinsella. He was, for the brief moment in my arms, substantial. A solid man, larger than me but not, after all, the towering figure of my imagination. At least not physically. But he looms over most of what I write, much of what I read, and everything I hope to be as a writer.

Oddly enough, in the fourteen years since I got sick, my poetry has undergone a thorough change. With my powers of concentration shredded, my abstract reasoning capacity sharply limited, my capacity to organize thoughts unreliable, the writing of poetry has become much more open for me. The poems are less formal, less cohesive, because my world and my mind are less cohesive. They are more like acts of discovery than acts of revelation, since I seldom know where my poems are going. It is a change I never could have imagined for myself before, something that wouldn't have happened until the lived life made it necessary.

**part three** *Turning Up the Gravity*

# 10  The Seafood Festival Talent Show

My wife and I had been singing "At the Hop" all week, and I thought we were ready for the Seafood Festival Talent Show on Saturday night. But in a pub at the edge of a tiny village on an island off the west coast of Ireland, you can't be sure about the house band. So in case they didn't know this classic rock 'n' roll hit from thirty-seven years earlier, I was prepared to represent us, solo, with "Love Me Tender." A capella, if I had to.

We'd performed "At the Hop" in public once, back home in Oregon eighteen months earlier. It hadn't gone well. Beverly, who was working then as the office administrator for a Japanese construction firm, was responsible for setting up their 1992 Christmas party. Instead of a strolling magician, fortune teller, or musicians, as in previous years, she was asked to hire a karaoke deejay. Her colleagues went into rigorous private rehearsals, as though preparing themselves for an important ritual. The boss polished up the one song he could perform well in English, "I Left My Heart in San Francisco," and one of the managers reprised his signature number, "I've Got You Under My Skin." Representatives from other companies in the trade and employees of the state business development agency were invited to participate. It became a gala. Because of Beverly's role in all this, because we were soon to get married and she was going to leave the firm, because everyone was participating and because the sense of excitement around the office became contagious, she felt we ought to perform a number too.

"At the Hop" was my idea. The song had come out when I was a ten-year-old rock 'n' roll fanatic who spent hours lip-syncing in front of his bedroom mirror, strumming a baseball bat. I still remembered the lyrics, and "At the Hop" had the sort of narrow vocal range for a lead singer that I could sometimes handle. Beverly was willing to handle the doo-wop backup. Let's go!

I'd never sung with a karaoke machine before, but that didn't worry me. It should have. At that time, four years after I got sick, I was still in the earliest stages of rehabilitating myself, working hard to repair the damage to my neurological functioning. I'd mastered some tricks to help with remembering. I was improving my ability to manage multiple stimuli and to cope with distraction so that I could be in a public place and function socially. I was concentrating for longer periods of time, strengthening my ability to patch together fragments of thought; walking awkwardly, with a cane; reading literature again and even writing again, which was very encouraging. But I hadn't been to a party in four years. Party? I hadn't been awake past 9:30 p.m. in four years. I wasn't sure I could remember my own name under these circumstances, let alone manage to sing.

Memory is a system; its parts sometimes work better separately than together. By the time Beverly and I were preparing for our karaoke debut, I'd understood from personal experience that certain kinds of memory—like the memory for lyrics or for poems learned by heart in the fifth grade or for how to ride a bicycle—can endure intact while other kinds of memory—like the name of your best childhood friend or what your daughter's telephone number might be—can vanish in a flash. Encoded differently in the first place, and stored in other parts of the brain, those often banal task memories can persist while important event memories evaporate.

I knew "At the Hop" cold, but didn't trust myself. So when it came time for us to perform in front of Beverly's colleagues and friends, I decided to watch the karaoke monitor and sing along with the scrolling lyrics, just to be safe. But concentrating on two things at once, asking my brain to process both internal and external versions of the same words, proved to be impossible. The ball bouncing over the words on the screen didn't keep pace with the song's rhythm or with the frantic pace of my crazed singing and I was quickly lost. The few lyrics I managed to utter were garbled and it didn't take long for the gap between lyrics and melody to become a chasm filled only by Beverly's backup singing. I then did the only thing that made sense to me at the moment: I put the microphone down on top of the machine and exited stage left, abandoning Beverly to continue singing background doo-wop sounds in her gorgeous alto while I hid in the kitchen, shamefaced among the sushi chefs. Her normally reserved Japanese bosses had never witnessed such a profound breach of karaoke etiquette before. Through the remainder of the party, they kept visiting our table to point at me and, struggling for control, say, "Ha-ha-ha, you walk off and leave wife!"

We'd been in Ireland for about two weeks now, staying at the Heinrich Böll Cottage on Achill Island, where I'd been granted that month-long writing residency. Böll, the German novelist who won a Nobel Prize for Literature in 1972, had lived and worked in the cottage for more than two decades. His family recently began allowing its use for artists' residencies and we were among the first Americans to find our way there. It was a sprawling, sparely furnished, four-bedroom structure with a peat-burning fireplace and abstracts in reds and browns painted by Böll's son, Rene, covering some of the walls. Böll's bedroom was plain, its windows overgrown by tangled brush, a shelf of his books in German above our heads.

I had a view of the sea from Böll's writing desk, at least in theory. According to a description in his book, *Irish Journal*, if the rain and clouds ever went away, and if I trimmed the masses of blooming fuchsia, "the blue tongue of the sea" would be pointing right at me.

It was early July, 1994, and only technically summer. The island's cold winds made us feel as though we'd brought Oregon winter along with our books, heavy clothing, granola, and canned tuna. Sunk below the level of the road and backed up against a 698-foot mountain named Krinnuck, Böll's cottage was the last domicile at the western tip of Dugort, a village of fewer than two hundred residents boasting a beautiful sand beach no one was brave enough to use in early July. If it weren't for the Seafood Festival, tourists wouldn't start coming to Achill until much later in the month.

Festival events were spread over the course of ten days and scattered across the island. It was difficult to imagine hitting a golf ball into the Achill winds, but there was a Seafood Festival Open Golf Competition on the first weekend. There was also shore angling and a duck race on the sandbanks at Keel, a yawl race in Achill Sound, a Deserted Village Walk starting at Dooagh Beach, an art exhibition in Currane—all too far for us to walk or cycle from our cottage, and none occurring in Dugort.

Most evenings since our arrival, we strolled two hundred yards from the cottage to the Slievemore Hotel's pub to sit near the door nursing a pint of stout and trying to breathe. Everyone smoked; I was sure that I'd seen a little boy in diapers with a cigarette stuck between his lips like a pacifier. A slender, bearded gentleman with thick eyeglasses and a leather cap pulled low over his forehead, sat at the bar's far corner, by the bathroom door, staring into an ashtray perched atop his pint glass. His gaze seemed professorial, and with his legs corkscrewed around each other on the barstool, arms crossed in front of his chest, hands under armpits, he looked as though he were struggling to hold himself together. We never saw him move. At the far end of the bar, opposite the professor, two brothers spent the whole month discussing Ireland's failed penalty kick in the latest World Cup soccer fiasco. A mother and her son were the rotating bartenders; along with a few regulars, they began to nod at us as the days wore on.

Built in 1839, the Slievemore was the island's oldest hotel, tucked off the road and up against the base of Slievemore itself, a 2,204-foot windswept mountain that dominates Achill's landscape. The hotel is seldom featured in tourist information, overshadowed by The Golden Strand, so it was a quiet haven. Patrons were used to a new writer showing up from the Böll place monthly, but those writers were usually Irish or German. A pair of Yanks was rare and they forgave me for not knowing that Smithwick's Beer was pronounced Smithix or that potato chips were crisps.

I saw the poster for the talent show when we were at the pub to watch the soccer games with the locals. It was scheduled for 9:00 Saturday night and, I read, it was to be one of the climactic events of an annual festival in "celebration of the fine quality seafood caught in the waters off Achill." Posters also turned up on a pole that held the mailbox near our cottage, and in the small shop across from Dugort Strand. At first we thought it would be fun to have a couple pints and watch the show. But then I began to see it as a chance to redeem myself from the earlier karaoke disaster. Virtually anonymous, scheduled to leave the island in a few weeks, an American and therefore someone from whom the worst could be expected—I had nothing to lose.

I kept this idea to myself. Beverly, I believe, never imagined that I'd actually sign us up for the talent show. Never subject myself to another round of public humiliation. She sang with me all week for the delight of song; only I considered what we were doing to be, potentially, rehearsal.

I grew up in a family where talent was granted by proclamation. My mother was in charge of the process, which was in essence a public relations campaign. Though her performing career stalled after her brief run as a radio singer, she believed that any child bearing her genes was, *ipso facto*, an artistic genius and would have the public acclaim she'd unfairly been denied.

A child who drew was declared the next Picasso until his drawings started to look like something recognizable, at which point he became the next Rembrandt. Receiving a guitar for my birthday transformed me into the new Segovia, though I'd had no lessons and lacked a scintilla of aptitude. When I rehearsed my Bar Mitzvah portion, I was a young (and still soprano) Sinatra. Such confidence in my gifts might seem encouraging, but unfortunately I was made to demonstrate them in public. By age seven, I was used to singing and dancing badly for an audience, handing my latest report card over to strangers, reading aloud and with elaborate dramatic emphasis from *The Story of Babar.* I gave strange command performances, modeling my new pajamas or saying my bedtime prayer in the living room for company. I was a performer well before I had anything to offer an audience, and I knew exactly how bad my act was. At thirteen, I finally refused to be put on display for her ever again. My announcement, during a family dinner the next night, was actually one of my better performances of the season.

But on my own, like a vaudeville lifer, I couldn't help volunteering to take a microphone. In 1959, at age twelve, I willingly declaimed Walt Whitman's poem, "O Captain! My Captain! " over the public address system at summer camp, in an effort to whip my Green Team into a frenzy as it went out to combat the Gray Team in baseball during the annual Color War. I wasn't sure how "my Captain lying fallen cold and dead" was supposed to inspire the team, but I'd agreed to read the thing and had been trained by my mother to make sure the show went on. From inside the Head Counselor's shack, I could hear my voice reverberate among the pines and didn't care for the awkward, squawky sound of it. Now, forty-six years later and despite the ravages of brain damage, I can still recall those stirring, totally inappropriate lines from a poem about the assassination of Abraham Lincoln: "But O heart! heart! heart!/O the bleeding drops of red,/Where on the deck my Captain lies,/Fallen cold and dead."

Also at summer camp, I eagerly auditioned for a role in *West Side Story* and was cast as A-Rab. At the director's urging, I learned to sing my part of "Officer Krupke" with an accent that fluctuated between stage German and Pennsylvania Dutch. During a unit on biographies in a high school English class, I was given the choice of writing a book report or performing something illustrative of my subject before the class. I made

Dr. Albert Schweitzer sound a lot like A-Rab in my presentation of his work in French Equatorial Africa.

Through two crucial years of my childhood, 1955 to 1957, my family's Sunday nights were sacrosanct. We might visit relatives in the afternoon, or eat early dinner at a restaurant, but we were home in time to gather around the television and watch Ted Mack's *Original Amateur Hour.* It was approached with the awe and anticipation that most families like ours reserved for Friday night Sabbath ceremonies. We turned the room lights off, sat in a semi-circle before the Philco, and no one was permitted to talk. *The Original Amateur Hour* was our family's essential myth given visible form: Talented Unknown Discovered And Proclaimed By Vote Of Entire Country!

Formerly a beloved radio program, beginning in the mid-1930s and hosted by a Major Bowes, *The Original Amateur Hour* was eventually brought to television by Mack, who had been Bowes' director and chief talent scout. Frank Sinatra was the most renowned discovery from the radio days. Since coming to television in 1948, it had become so popular that in 1955 ABC moved the program into its Sunday night lineup.

Broadcast from Radio City Music Hall, it brought contestants to New York and gave them a few minutes to perform on live television. Mack spun a wheel of fortune, saying, "Round and around she goes, and where she stops nobody knows," to determine the weekly contestants' stakes. Viewers would call or write to select winners, who would then be brought back for further competitions. It was possible to win three times, accumulating cash prizes or scholarships or even parts in a stage show sponsored by the program. Prizes were incidental in my mother's view; she was rapt by the possibility that a person could appear on national television, could become famous and return to double and even triple acclaim. His or her talents could be revealed for all to see, fair and square, sudden and stunning. Exactly the sort of chance she'd been denied.

Unlike *Arthur Godfrey's Talent Scouts*, which featured professional contestants, Ted Mack's show was strictly for amateurs.

And it showed. With its often terrible singers and musicians, its dancers and novelty acts, *The Original Amateur Hour* was a precursor to Chuck Barris' *The Gong Show*. Few contestants got invited back for a second appearance. But occasionally, someone special would appear: Pat Boone and Teresa Brewer got their starts on Ted Mack's program; an eight-year-old Gladys Knight, sans Pips, won by singing Brahms' "Lullaby" and Nat King Cole's "Too Young"; a teenaged Penny Marshall appeared with several friends in a dance troupe; Ann-Margret first appeared before the American public on *The Original Amateur Hour*, but wasn't a winner. And if these people, none of whom were my mother's children or connected to her by blood, could be discovered, it followed that I could too. All I needed was a little more seasoning.

Beverly knew none of this history as we sang "At the Hop" while cooking dinners in the Heinrich Böll Cottage. If she had, she might not have been so willing to humor me, or to look past my abandonment of her on the karaoke stage. She was the one in our family with real singing talent; she was also the one who liked to avoid public performance, agreeing to participate in a Christmas Choir back home only as part of a large, similarly dressed team, where she could sing for the joy of it while disappearing into the group.

Because we only brought what would fit in one backpack each, Beverly and I had been rigorous in our choices. I'd filled a gallon-size plastic storage bag with Starbucks ground decaffeinated coffee, brought along a small packet of filters and a plastic single-cup filter holder. I planned to nurse the supply along and buy something locally when it ran out. But I'd finished the Starbucks in a week, marching from Böll's writing room to his kitchen and back as I struggled to write the old-fashioned way again, with pens and paper instead of a computer or even a typewriter. I didn't mind the slow pace of the work, but I did seem to require a lot more time to pace. And prepare coffee one cup at a time. There was no local stock of ground coffee, only small jars of instant, which was not going to get me through the remainder of our residency. So during my first phone conversation with our house sitter back in Oregon, I accepted his offer—originally dismissed as unnecessary—to send me four pounds of Starbucks via FedEx.

He sent it out the next morning, but a week later, the coffee still hadn't arrived. All this, I told myself, was good for me. It was crazy to need Starbucks coffee on Achill Island! We'd come here to immerse ourselves in the place, to live without a car or computers or a music system or showers or most of our customary conveniences, and enjoy the land, enjoy the people and culture and history. I'd write, Beverly would paint, and in the afternoons we'd explore. Walk on the lower slopes of Slievemore; enjoy the high cliffs at Minaun and Keem Bay, where the basking shark fisheries used to be; go into Dugort and spend time on the strand; see the bare, haunting seafront graveyard where unbaptized children were buried in the past; bike five miles for groceries or other necessities. So much to do, and I was worried about my decaf.

Some people have a talent for roughing it. Or for semi-roughing it, which is what life on Achill seemed like to me, though our accommodations at the cottage and conditions on the island weren't really primitive. Beverly, who grew up in a family that took annual fishing trips to rugged, remote Canadian locations; who loved to camp and hike and kayak in rivers; who had lived alone for four years in the small house she built in the middle of twenty hidden acres of woods before I joined her there; who had lived in an isolated Scottish village for four years during the 1980s; felt fully at ease in our situation. She painted in a back room of the cottage filled with light, even in the rain, singing as she worked. She was eager for whatever the day brought us, glad to be tromping through the heather, stopping at a pub near Dookinella for a game of pool, allowing the aged owner of a gem shop to flirt shamelessly with her while we admired his amethyst collection.

The longer we were on the island, though, and the more I followed Beverly's lead, the more comfortable I became with a way of life that had seemed at first to be rooted in the late

Victorian era. I'd believed I was *sacrificing* in order to have this experience of writing in Ireland. After all, I hadn't brought along a coffee machine.

One of our favorite walks was along the crest of Krinnuck, which rose directly behind the cottage and sloped down toward the sea. I'd been trying to learn how to walk for brief periods without a cane, slowly building up confidence and strength, trying to compensate for my unpredictable sense of balance. Climbing up the hill, I found that my cane was useless because at every step it sank into the soggy ground. Beverly encouraged me to let her hold the cane and walked beside me on the right—my cane side—to provide a visual sense of support. I soon relaxed, noticing the heather and bog cotton, calling to the cows that watched our approach. If we walked when I was feeling rested and alert, things went well. I was able to walk on my own for longer periods as the month went on, braced by Beverly's love and confidence. On the day of the talent show, as I made it to the locked gates of the deserted Protestant church, a half hour's walk, I felt as though my whole sense of what I was doing on Achill had begun to come clear.

In the first, acute year of my illness, I had been silenced as a writer by the damage to my brain. I couldn't imagine that I'd be capable of composing a poem or story again. But writing came back, initially in brief notes and scattered sentences, in images or a flickering thought. Well into the second year, and for the first time in my life as a writer, I began writing essays. Fragmented, associative, explorative, but nevertheless prose I believed to cohere as actual essays. Being able to write again, even in fragments, seemed to me a kind of rebirth. A year later, with the help of Thomas Kinsella, I was granted this residency in Ireland and, though no obligations were placed on me to write new work, I felt it essential to be productive while there.

But at the far end of Krinnuck, sitting beside Beverly with my back against the gates of the church, I understood that I was there to extend the renewal that had begun with my fragmentary writing. I'd been lifted from the familiar surroundings of my world and given a chance to see new things, or old things in new ways. Including myself. I was in a place where it made sense to distance myself from memories of humiliation at my neurological failings. I was writing a little, walking without a cane for a few minutes at a time, learning from Beverly how to revel in the simple life we'd stumbled into. I didn't need Starbucks. I didn't need my computer. I might not even need to sing "At the Hop" that night.

Because it's so far north, Achill's summer light lingers until almost 11:00. So when we left the cottage a little after 8:30 on Saturday night and headed for the pub, it felt as though we were taking an early afternoon stroll. Though I'd been napping during the days and staying awake later at night, my sense of time on the island had come loose. I was often disoriented, but as Beverly liked to remind me, coming loose isn't always a bad thing.

Sheep had congregated as usual on the road, their fleece marked by strips of red or blue paint. They sashayed in the general direction of Krinnuck, offering the occasional comment as we wound our way among them. I glanced over at the hill and saw two huge cows standing on its top, gazing out at the sea like tourists too tired by their long climb to bother with a photograph. *We'll remember this*, their long stare suggested.

The pub was nearly empty. I'd been concerned about getting there too late to find a table. But by 9:00—the official start time for the talent show—only the Professor, the brothers still sorting out Ireland's World Cup defeat, two families with children in tow, the bartender, and the band were there with us. Maybe I'd gotten the time wrong? That wouldn't be a real surprise. I walked to the bar and noticed a sign-up sheet near the Professor's elbow. On top, in red ink, it said TALENT SHOW 9:00, and there were dozens of thick black lines drawn below two headings: NAME and PERFORMING. Otherwise, the sheet was blank. I left it that way, ordered our pints, and rejoined Beverly at the table we'd chosen for a clear view of the show.

Band members and their friends clustered near an impromptu stage by the pub's eastern wall. They pushed a couple of tables together and began an elaborate series of movements that almost seemed choreographed, a dreamy sarabande that would continue for the next two hours. First, the guitarist drifted onstage and played two quick riffs, then sat down; next the drummer went to check his kit, slashed at the cymbals, and returned to the table; the keyboard player patted the drummer's shoulder and walked onstage, bent to peer under his instrument and check various connections, then played a few notes of a song that might have been "A Whole New World" but was over before I could be sure. After he sat down at the table, the singer walked onstage, flipped some switches, slapped the microphone, said, "Testing two three four," and returned to the table. Finally they all raised their glasses and drank.

I went to the bathroom at around 10:00 and, on my way back, glanced at the sign-up sheet. There were two names on it, but I didn't pause long enough to decipher their proposed performances because if anyone had noticed, I might feel compelled to add our names. The pub was almost half full now. It seemed crammed because of the smoke and laughter, the constant movement of people from group to group.

"Did you sign up?" Beverly asked.

I smiled as though that were the furthest thing from my mind. "There's no rush."

At about 10:30, with the pub full and dozens of wee children drifting among tables, the singer looked around after "Testing two three four" and coughed. He tugged at his black cowboy hat, smiled, waved toward the Professor, and urged us all to participate in the talent show. Then, to my shock, the rest of the band joined him onstage. Beverly and I figured this would be the opening set.

"We'd like to do a little number now by Garth Brooks," the singer said. The band was good, but the singer's voice was flat and sour, which gave me great hope. He sang "Friends in Low

Places," waved back at the applauding crowd, and the band returned to their seats.

A half hour later, they got up to sing Brooks' new ballad, "The Dance," and sat down again. Near 11:00 I noticed two elderly men leaning over the sign-up sheet and, on my way to the bathroom again, looked to see what they'd written. There were thick dark lines drawn through both names that had been on the sheet.

The band played "Friends in Low Places" again and at midnight, Beverly and I gave up, left the Slievemore and walked back to the cottage. It was, finally, dark outside; we headed into a lacerating, wind-driven rain, clutching each other's arms and laughing. We could hear, but not see cattle somewhere off to the south. Then I heard Beverly humming close to my ear. It was a melody I recognized, so I began to mumble the lyrics, calling on all cats and chicks to go to the hop. We, on the other hand, were going to bed.

Maybe the talent show would still take place. But when we'd left the pub, there were still only two names on the sign-up sheet, both of them crossed out.

# 11 The Song of the Exhausted Well

I didn't know Beverly had left our bed till I heard her say "Oh, no," from behind the bathroom door. She is not a woman who says, *Oh, no.* I was instantly awake in the early morning light.

"What's wrong?"

"We're out of water again. I can't believe this."

My first thought: maybe this is a dream. My second thought: I filled the Brita pitcher last night; it can't be out of water already.

But I knew in my heavy heart exactly what she meant. She'd turned on the tap at the sink and nothing came out. When it happens to me, I always turn the tap off quickly, wait a few seconds and try again, a truly idiotic reaction. Then I try the bath and run upstairs to see if maybe the kitchen faucet will work, unable to accept that no water truly means no water.

The barren tap, I have come to see, is one of the rural dweller's signature horror moments, right up there with spooky goings-on deep in the woods. When I was growing up in our Brooklyn apartment in the 1950s, and maintenance problems occurred, we called the building superintendent. But there's no super here in the woods. There's just us. And our unreliable water supply.

This particular morning in 2001 the barren tap seemed a compound horror, a clear sign of spooky goings-on deep in the woods. The absence of water struck me as the land's sound of pure negation, because less than a year before we'd spent fifteen thousand dollars to drill a new well. After years and years of turning on taps to find the water gone, of practicing ruthless conservation, we'd finally given up on the old well, with its capacity dwindling down below a quarter gallon a minute.

The waterless days were supposed to be over. I HAD A RECEIPT!

We were married in this house in the late spring of 1993. Because it's so small, we could only invite family and a very few friends to join us—two dozen people, including the husband-and-wife chaplain team that performed the ceremony. Still, during the course of the party they managed enough toilet flushes to run the old well dry for the night.

Beverly and I refused to see this as some kind of sign. It had nothing to do with our marriage or the romantic beauty of living in this isolated house we called *Casa Amor*. After all, the well had never been very good. Drilled to two hundred ninety feet, it originally yielded only four gallons of water a minute. That was just barely enough for Beverly to qualify for a mortgage. But others on the hill were getting twenty, thirty, forty-five gallons a minute from wells that were much shallower. At thirty dollars per foot, the only consolation for having to drill so deep would be a generous yield from the well. But she had the worst of both—a much deeper well than anyone around, yielding a fraction of the water.

Our first investment as a married couple was a thousand-gallon water storage tank. The theory was clear enough: our new tank would fill slowly, at a pace the well could tolerate, and we'd draw water from it without directly taxing the water source. A thousand gallons in storage would be plenty for us. A rule of thumb is that a person uses about two hundred fifty gallons a day for showers, cooking, washing. We would never use so much water that the well couldn't replenish it during the down times.

After the tank was installed, I had a dream in which the great poet T. S. Eliot came to examine our land. He was mumbling, speaking in that odd pseudo-British accent of his, but as he walked across the gravel driveway I recognized passages from *The Waste Land*: "Here is no water but only rock," he said.

"Rock and no water." Then he approached the shed we'd built to accommodate the water storage tank and raised a hand. It might have been a gesture of blessing or of warning. Then he spoke again: "If there were the sound of water only . . . Drip drop drip drop drop drop drop . . . But there is no water."

I began rereading *The Waste Land*, looking for clues. Maybe Eliot's blessing was the warning. Over the next few years, Beverly and I bought a front-loading washing machine acclaimed for its low water usage and stopped using the dishwasher. We put a special head on the shower guaranteed to be a water miser, and mastered the art of speed showering: the flow turned off while lathering, the rinse quick as a baptism. We adopted a toilet-flush policy summarized as *if it's yellow, let it mellow, if it's brown, flush it down,* a lyric that the younger Eliot might have admired. We no longer refilled the small pond Beverly installed for her water plants, which the deer used as their personal drinking fountain and salad bar. We removed the submersible, wood-burning stove from the hot tub and gave up moonlight soaks. Inch by inch, year by year, Beverly narrowed the perimeter of grass in the small back yard, designing a more ragged look with lots of bark dust and plants that thrived in drought conditions. Since watering a lawn uses so much water, we watched the remaining patch of grass turn yellow under July and August sun. She gave up planting thirsty annuals and our summer vegetable garden. We bought a solar shower, a huge black bladder we could fill when water was available, then allow the sun to heat for a fast, awkward wash when the well was down. We stocked our small storage room with containers of distilled drinking water for emergency use, and smaller jugs with tap water for refilling a flushed toilet. For even more desperate times, we found a portable toilet seat we could take into the woods and place on a tripod under the shade of a gnarled oak. Beside it, we stashed a bucket of ash from our wood stove. We also had a few buckets handy in case the well went dry during the four or five months when the winter creek was dribbling along, and two bottles with built-in filters that could make creek water potable.

We became, in short, water maniacs. Driving past a field in the valley below our hill, we saw farms being irrigated sloppily and took it personally, watching as water that might otherwise have been in our aquifer cascaded onto the highway or evaporated in the mid-afternoon glare. When we traveled, we became giddy over motel showers with good water pressure.

But no matter how diligently we conserved, the well was tiring out. More and more often, we'd turn on taps and there would be nothing, not even a trickle. *If there were the sound of water only!* When there was water, it was often rank with minerals even though we had an iron filter and water softener system in place. We added a Brita filter to our kitchen faucet and had to replace it almost monthly, and used a Brita pitcher to double-filter our drinking water. In the washing machine, white clothing turned a range of shades between cream and amber. Showering in hard water scented my skin of deep earth; I thought of it as a new cologne: eau-de-terre. The pump inside our well began to wear out as it worked to supply water when there was none to draw. Eventually, the pump's shutoff mechanism burned itself and the motor died. Soon the automatic cycling that was intended to fill our water storage tank during hours of low demand began to fail as well, and we had to experiment with manual operations whenever water seemed to be present. We got to know the pump repairman, with his unpredictable moods like a reflection of our water system.

Western Oregon, where we live, is famous for being a wet place. It's supposed to rain all the time here, to be so misty and cloudy that everyone is depressed from October through June. Oregonians talk fervently of mold and fungus. Wetness is ingrained in our culture. Early settlers wrote poems celebrating the drenched landscape, such as Valentine Brown's 1904 verse in which the voice of the Chinook Wind promised to "bring a green mantle for hillside and lea." Sixty years later, Ken Kesey's *Sometimes a Great Notion*, set mostly in western Oregon, began with a prologue featuring "the hysterical crashing of tributaries" and "a vast smile of water," evoking a landscape where "the sky runs gray, the smoke wet-yellow." Out here you can buy Oregon Rain eyeglasses and Oregon Rain soap and Oregon Rain bath salts. Our state insect is the Oregon rain beetle and even the mascots of the state's three universities are all water-related: the Ducks, the Beavers, the Vikings.

How can wells run dry in Oregon, a state with a hundred and twelve thousand miles of rivers and streams? There are more than six thousand lakes and there are the great snow-capped Cascade peaks—Mt. Hood, Mt. Jefferson, Mt. Bachelor—providing meltwater in spring.

But the truth is that the climate where Beverly and I live is almost Mediterranean, which is why the growing of grapes for winemaking has become such a vital industry. It might rain often, but it doesn't rain a lot, and the rain feels like heavy mist. There's little or no precipitation in summer, which is typically a time of yellowed grasses, cracked soil, dust devils, wildfires.

The hill we live on is made mostly of basalt from old lava flows, and basalt doesn't hold moisture as well as grainy soil types. Beverly knows her geology, having majored in the subject as an undergraduate, and we've studied the story our land tells. This hill was formed in late Miocene time, when great sheets of basaltic lava poured through the Columbia gorge and reached this area, eventually forming the slopes of the Amity Hills. We live on dark, crystalline columns of basalt almost a thousand feet thick. It is not water-friendly ground.

So given the landscape, climate, and agriculture around us, what we were experiencing with our exhausted well—which had never been adequate to begin with—wasn't a total surprise. But that didn't make it any less of a shock actually to run out of water.

According to the original 1988 Well Water Report filed with the state by Marv Grayson, the well constructor, the first four feet through which he had to dig was made up of boulders. These aren't just big rocks; they're enormous otherworldly masses that bring to mind asteroids rather than stones. Remnants of Ice Age floods, these glacial erratics might have landed on our hill after a slow trip west from Montana. Below the boulders, Marv found more than forty feet of diced basalt and then another thirty feet of hard, weathered basalt. Then came deep layers of hard, dark shale. When water, even at only four gallons a minute, was finally found at two hundred ninety feet, Beverly told him to stop there because she'd run out of funds. Finally done with the well, Marv told Beverly he never would have taken the job if he'd known what was down there.

But he came back, armed with new equipment, when we called twelve years later. Walking with us past the old well, Marv stopped and took off his hat. I thought he was performing some kind of well constructor's funeral ritual, but he was only trying to scratch his scalp.

"I remember this one, all right," he said, shaking his head, sighing. Then, with great tact, he added, "Maybe we ought to drill the new well some distance from here."

We walked the land with him, talking about site factors. He needed adequate room to bring in two rigs, the drill itself on one truck and its sidekick on a long flatbed that carried an array of other equipment. The rig was tall, so there couldn't be trees overhead. He also needed a manageable slope and an area down which the muddy effluent could flow, where its unsightly lingering mess would not be visible.

All this led us to a section of woods just off the narrow gravel drive, about halfway between the road and our house. It was where I liked to enter the woods for my afternoon walks, almost flat for a few dozen yards, most of the fir and oak slightly thinner than elsewhere on the twenty acres. Marv put his arms out in front of his chest, then spread them in a semi-circle like a swimmer doing the breaststroke.

"Somewhere in here, maybe."

I nodded sagely and asked, "So you think there's water down here?"

Marv shrugged. "Should be."

Then he was talking about the other wells on our hill, and in the valley below, and it seemed as though he thought the signs were good. But you don't drill a well *somewhere*. You drill a well in one specific place and it's a real crapshoot. A thirty-dollar-per-foot crapshoot. You'd think there would be more science to it.

Marv had a good sense of where his work would be most efficient and the land's contours looked all right to him. But because homes were so scattered around here, there weren't enough wells to suggest a pattern for where the water might be. No one, apparently, could say exactly where Marv should start drilling.

Beverly and I had been talking about just this problem. Back in 1988, she'd hired a dowser to divine the presence of hidden water for her. Though the dowser did locate a site, she hadn't acted immediately. Instead, camping by herself at various places throughout the undeveloped land, she waited for some further sign. Waking one morning in thick mist, she saw a deer standing exactly where the dowser had said the water would be. This seemed like a good sign.

The problem was, the dowser and the deer had found a site that wasn't very good and that had dried up within twelve years. But we knew that other factors, beyond the ken of dowsers and deer, had contributed to the well's downfall. We'd been discussing whether to hire another dowser; I had doubts about divining the location of water by using a stick, just as I'd had doubts about astrology and naturopathic medicine. But I do behave like a typical Cancer and naturopathy has helped. So after seeing how limited the other approaches to finding water were, and after Marv suggested that we try this dowser he knew, I was ready for any extra help. In fact, I was hoping that my mantra cadged from *The Waste Land* would make a difference when added to the dowser's magic and properly aligned stars. *Drip drop drip drop drop drop drop.*

Jake Emery opened the rear of his hatchback and released two frothing dogs who chased our cats into trees. This didn't feel like a good sign. Jake laughed and held out his hand, saying, "Don't worry, they're harmless."

The dogs pissed on the trees, then headed off into the woods. Jake smiled at them like a proud father.

He was eighty, tall and lean, and said he could already sense something promising about this land of ours. A round house, huh? Must be nice living in a home without sharp edges.

He carried his dowsing gear in a leather quiver slung over his right shoulder as we walked up toward the site Marv had chosen. Jake's load was light; inside the quiver was a wire coat hanger unfurled into a U shape and a couple of thin, forked fir limbs. He plucked out the hanger and let it dangle from his right hand.

We explained our aqua-history but Jake didn't seem to be listening. About halfway up the drive, as though summoned west by the folding landscape, he veered left and entered the woods, heading straight to the spot where Marv had spread his arms. Beverly and I looked at each other. Had the two men talked so that Jake would know roughly where to go?

He studied the ground, the trees, the rocks. His pale blue eyes seemed to darken toward sapphire and he suddenly looked half his age. He flexed his knees. The breeze disappeared, making the air feel clearer.

"There are signs everywhere," he said. "Obvious things that most of us simply miss."

"Like what?" I asked.

"Anything can be a sign. Smell those blooming lilies? They tell you something."

"So what about the water?"

He shrugged. "Don't worry, it's all around here. You know, I can find anything I put my mind to." He turned to face us and said it was all about hidden fields of force that call to those who listen. Haven't we ever seen animals know a storm is coming before the signs are clear to us? Aren't we animals too? We've just gotten out of touch with this primitive way of knowing. "People doubt dowsing, but they don't doubt music is nothing but waves of sound plucked from the sky, or color is light disturbed before the eye can find it. Why not the same with water, with anything? I once located a lost child in the woods by feeling his agitation in the air. I stopped hunting when I realized it wasn't fair, I could track prey too easily. Same with fishing. And I can tell when there's joy, too." He held his hanger up before his chest, its tips pointed toward me and Beverly, and we all saw it twitch. "Just fields of force," he said.

What the hell was this? Was Jake conning us, or was he somehow for real? I wished he'd just find our water, mark the spot, take his hundred dollars cash, and leave, because my faith was wavering.

It's good, I decided. Jake's mysticism can combine with geology and the knowledge of existing well patterns, with Marv's practical well-drilling savvy and with T. S. Eliot's poetry, and we'll have all our bases covered.

Jake turned away from us and began tracing a meandering line of hidden water. He walked slowly, arms loose, senses alert, hydro-stalking. This part I liked; the man was getting down to business. He tied orange ribbons to overhanging limbs and marked off several points along which Marv might drill. Then he mumbled something to his coat hanger, which vibrated a bit before pointing straight down.

"Here you go," he said. "It's a strong source too. No more than a hundred fifty feet down there." He drove a stake into the spot.

Come on, we were supposed to believe he knew how deep the water was? Not just where, but how deep? What next, the mineral content? I didn't see anything different about the spot he'd picked; I didn't hear anything. Oh, I thought. *If there were the sound of water only!*


A few days before Marv was scheduled to begin the new well, Hubert Cobb showed up with his bulldozer. Douglas fir and oak overhanging the site would interfere with the drilling rig, and had to be removed. Smaller trees had to come out too, and the large boulders that had heaved up above the ground needed to be cleared.

Hubert waved to me from the dozer's seat and smiled as he entered the woods. Clearly, he loved working with the equipment and clearing things up. He worked fast, roaring forwards and backwards through the woods. But soon he wasn't smiling anymore. I could hardly keep him in focus as he bounced in his seat. The rubbled land tossed his machine around and he looked like a cowboy working a nasty bucking bronco. He kept at it, though, face covered in muck, hat flopping.

"Never have seen anything like this ground you got," he shouted. "Been thumped around so much, I think my kidneys moved up under my shoulder blades."

By mid-afternoon, Hubert was gone and the site had a bombed-out look, trees down, roots dangling in the air. Some had been shoved to the edge of the site and lay tangled there among boulders caked with mud. There was a feeling of sudden, glaring light where no light had shined for ages, of harsh exposure, though in truth only a small patch of the woods was changed. Hubert had freed an arc large enough for the two trucks and cleared a pathway for the effluent. As a favor, he'd then taken his machine down near the old vegetable garden and shoved aside five years worth of blackberry vines. We were all set.

Marv arrived with the morning light. But it didn't stay light for long because rain moved in, the year's first September rain. We decided that rain on drilling day was a very good sign, even if Marv didn't seem pleased. Beverly was ready to spend the morning intensely visualizing water. Nice water, lots of water, and not too deep. I was ready to recite Eliot.

We went up to greet Marv and his team, then back to the house to let them work. We could hear the racket of their various power sources, but could only see them from the tiny window above our kitchen sink. We tried not to stand there all day monitoring progress.

Most of the morning Marv and his helper were setting things up. They backed the drill truck into the woods and positioned it where Jake had left his stake, then used struts to level the vehicle. All that afternoon, all that evening, all the next day, I had a clear view of the truck reared up like some monstrous horse on those black struts. Shivering and roaring, the drill disgorged sludge. Blown rock ripped through the trees beyond the site, stripping leaves as the air filled with mist that was a shade darker than café au lait. The runoff was rimmed with muddy foam swirls as it drifted down over the hill's sharp folds. We could often see a link of steel casing dangling from its winch above the well hole.

When Marv went beyond the one hundred fifty foot mark that Jake and his coat hanger had predicted, my heart sank. By day's end, the only water Marv had found was the rain. The deepening black hole up there was looking like a chasm into which all our money would disappear.

On the second morning, just as Marv began work, I had a clarifying vision. Looking out the kitchen window, I saw that the configuration of equipment looked just like the scene in Eliot's poem: "Upside down in air were towers/ Tolling." The sound it made wasn't bells, but to my crazed ears it suggested cacophonous "voices singing out of empty cisterns and exhausted wells." Something was going on there, because the key elements from *The Waste Land*'s climax were visible right beside my driveway.

I felt that I had to follow the path Eliot laid out for me. When it came to dry land, this poet understood. It was time to move toward full acceptance, toward "the awful daring of a moment's surrender" before the invisible "controlling hands." Because, I thought, water turns where it will underground. Its hidden path is ours to follow only with luck and blessings from the heavens and from the past stacked in its layers below ground. Maybe the water Jake felt had sunk closer to the earth's core because I hadn't believed properly. By doubting the dowser and his art, I'd compromised his quest to help us. And now, in the September wind and rain overwhelmed by the riot of the driller's rig, I imagined that I was finally hearing the music, the grave song of all the world's exhausted wells.

Maybe this well-drilling experience was a test. Or rather, a lesson. My mantra, I understood, should not be *drip drop drip drop drop drop drop*, but Eliot's final words in the poem, that ancient cry of peace in the desiccated world: *Shantih shantih shantih.*

Marv did finally find us water. At four hundred ninety-five feet. About a hundred feet earlier, he'd come down to the house to tell us the unthinkable: this might be a dry hole. But we'd have to pay the going rate anyway, so we agreed with him and chose to go a little deeper. Within an hour, we heard something magical happen: silence. Marv had shut off the drill. When I looked through the kitchen window, his smile was huge and white in the middle of his muddied face.

Now we had water, and though it only measured eight gallons a minute—still substantially less than the worst well anywhere else on this hill—it would be enough for our needs. As the work on the site concluded, and the well was linked to our water tank by a couple hundred yards of pipe, Beverly and I found ourselves moving together toward a positive way of looking at how it was all turning out. Yes, the well would cost almost three times what we had planned. Yes, it would not be as much water as we wished. But we were, as Marv informed us, into the deep aquifer. Into the place where water should be present for a very long time. We shouldn't be subjected to the vicissitudes of annual rainfall and snowmelt. We were, if we looked at this right, in good shape.

A little more than a year later, I woke up to Beverly's *oh, no.* We were out of water. This time, with our new fifteen thousand dollar well, the failure caught us less well prepared. We still had bottled drinking water, but only two jugs of tap water to use for flushing the toilet. The winter creek was dry. After calling the well repair team, we sat in the kitchen eating toast off paper plates and talked about selling the house and moving to Portland where there was a good city water supply. Enough with country living.

But this time we were more or less lucky. After opening the

well and pulling the pump from its home almost five hundred feet below, the repair team discovered that we were not, in fact, out of water. The well wasn't dry at all. But there had been a collapse of dirt down below the level of concrete casing, filling the well bottom and causing the pump to freeze up when it tried to pump water from mud. All we needed was a new pump. Not under warranty, naturally.

Now, several months later, Beverly and I find that our confidence has been deeply shaken. We'd allowed ourselves to think that maybe, just maybe, we had reliable water at last. But no, the point is that water is never reliable, and we're back to conserving our water.

This morning, going up the driveway to get our mail, I stopped to look at the wellhead and surrounding site. The arc of woods that Hubert cleared a year ago is still marked at its edges by the downed trees and rocky rubble, but that is not what draws the eye. The ground all around is green with wild grasses. There are patches of goldenrod, wooly sunflower, tansy and thistle, some of the weeds already in bloom and adding their yellow or purple flowers to the scene. Two boulders are lined up like a quarterback behind his hulking center, both gazing straight at the upright wellhead. The dry, caked path where effluent flowed downhill from the well site resembles an abandoned deer trail, if I look at it quickly enough. From certain angles, the whole site is almost beautiful. From other angles, it still looks like a war zone.

# 12  Thinking in Circles

"Oh my God," the man says. He is about seventy and tentatively balanced on one foot in our doorway as he tries to remove his left shoe while staring across the round room. He teeters a little, leans back against a wall, and smiles. "Will you just look at that?" Releasing his foot, he is oblivious to everything except the view through an arc of south-facing windows. "If I lived here," he whispers, "I'd never get anything done. I'd just gape at the woods."

He is at our house to see and, we hope, buy Beverly's art. For two weekends every October, we turn our tiny, cedar-sided yurt into a gallery. We hang about a dozen paintings on the walls, mount several more on small easels here and there, perch others against boxes on the kitchen counter or against the credenza on the living room floor. She is a painter of landscapes and still lifes, mostly in oil but sometimes in pastel or acrylic, the work informed as much by her early training in geology as by her later study of Impressionist styles and her spiritual practice.

These six days in mid-autumn, during the countywide Art Harvest Open Studio Tour, our home is taken over by the rich colors, forms, and textures of her work. And we open our isolated, normally tranquil place to all comers. That can be a deeply unsettling experience. We have only 615 square feet of circular space to work with, so it feels as crowded as the lobby of a concert hall at intermission. We bake banana bread and muffins, and I sit at the dining room table with an emptied tackle box to collect checks, a receipt book, and a price list.

The room's footprint during the tour is precarious. There

are obstacles everywhere. And the art, you would think, is hard to avoid. But this man, enraptured by the view, has woven his way over to our south-facing wall, which is nearly all glass, to look across the valley and into the Eola Hills.

"If you ever want to sell it, I'll buy this house," he says.

Beverly and I look at each other. During the tour, we have seen and heard this several times every hour. It is not a serious offer, we know that, but it feels strange now because—remarkable as it is, much as we love living here—we are talking again about selling our home and moving.

We are moving to the Oregon coast. We need to be near water and feel open, wild space around us.

After eleven years of living together in the woods of rural western Oregon, we feel utterly enclosed by our twenty acres of oak, maple, wild cherry, and Douglas fir. The forest is always trying to close in further too, relentless in its efforts to reclaim what has been cleared. If we have been away for a couple of weeks, we return to find things around the house a little tighter, vines sprawling closer to the house, grasses looming, tree limbs heavier and nearer, the few carefully nurtured flowers consumed by encroaching deer. Even when we are at home and our two aged cats are theoretically on-the-job, mice colonize the storage shed, nesting in boxes that contain old computer monitors or copies of now defunct magazines that published my poetry in the 1970s. Frogs take over the small pond Beverly built for her water plants, their mating calls keeping us awake all spring. The work of maintaining the house and land seems endless.

The land is too rocky for the gardening Beverly loves. A few years ago, when we built a small, enclosed gazebo for her to use as her art studio, Beverly prepared the site by digging a shallow trench for the electrical wiring. Every stroke of her shovel rang against rock and jarred her whole body. Gradually, the proposed site inched closer to the electrical power source in our water storage shed so she did not have to dig as far as planned. The man who drained our septic system this year vowed never to return after digging down two feet to the top of the tank.

"There's no dirt," he said. "Just rocks."

Living here has been a fifteen-year process of compromises with the implacable forces of solid earth, rock, and botany.

All of which seems intensified by the lack of water. Drought and our recent history with wells make us feel parched all the time, prevent us from growing our own vegetables, hem us in further during the brief season of Oregon sunlight. Weather and landscape, not human will, dictate what will thrive here.

Yes, we need to be by the open water. The coast! Where beaches are owned by the state and open to everyone. Where there is not only ocean but estuaries and rivers, even a few lakes. Space and light. The sound of waves, the briny scent, the taste and feel of salt in the air. It calls to us like the waters of Sligo called to William Butler Yeats as he stood before a London window-display, when he heard "lake water lapping with low sounds by the shore" and realized that "while I stand on the roadway, or on the pavements gray,/I hear it in the deep heart's core." That's us, all right, yearning for the sea.

We discuss the possibilities. Do not want to move too far from Portland, where Beverly's family has always lived, where my mother lives in a nursing home, where Powell's Bookstore is. Do not want to move to the tourist towns, Cannon Beach or Newport or Seaside, because we cannot imagine being around so many people after all these years in the woods. Do not want to live too close to Highway 101, with its traffic and noise drowning out the sound of the sea. Prefer free-standing home rather than development, the more remote the better. Pretty soon, it sounds like we just want to move our present house to a stand of woods at the coast.

Except we also need more space, more rooms. Beverly built this house when she lived alone, with no idea that someone would join her, bringing along his king-size bed and his books and his chair and his STUFF. Long ago, we reached critical mass, and every new acquisition—from a sewing table to a paperback book—requires that something else be off-loaded.

We spend several weekends driving up and down the coast. We try to zero in on possible areas, narrow our sights to the fifty-or-so miles between Lincoln City to the south and Manzanita to the north. Nothing further than two hours from Portland. We study real estate listings on line, look at newspapers, find a realtor in Manzanita and look at everything he has to show us.

But nothing seems quite right. For one thing, the wind at the coast is ferocious. When we ask the realtor if this is typical, he looks away, squints into the mist like an old salt, and admits that it is.

"The coast is a windy place. No getting away from that." He thinks for a moment, then offers a hopeful smile. "Famous for its storms, you know. People come from all over just to watch our storms."

He is right. Everywhere we look now we see evidence of what storm exposure can do. Salt spray and sand everywhere. Fretted, pitted stones and shrubs sculpted into the shape of the wind. Scalped capes, gouged headlands with one or two gnarled trees huddled on their desperate roots above a cove. It is difficult to walk the beach in late fall, in winter, early spring.

Even if we ignore the wind and dark, changeable weather, there is a problem with population density. The smaller towns are not really small, straggling as they do toward one another, testing the limits of growth. The land that can be built on has been built on; the whole stretch of fifty miles seems connected now, one long village separated by a few geological features that prohibit development. The more we look, the more we realize that the coast may be both too crowded and too open and wild for us. At the end of each house-hunting trip, we find ourselves delighted to be home.

Upstairs, Beverly is fiddling "Turkey in the Straw" in softening summer light. I sit at my desk in the room below, hearing her foot tap the beat, then both of her feet begin shuffling of their own accord. I lean back in my seat and can feel the way everything up there is coming together for her, the violin and her body becoming one integrated force, tones balancing, melody growing tighter. An easiness takes over and I can sense my spirits growing more buoyant as she plays.

I imagine her music filling the round room she is in, circling her lean figure where it bobs before the windows, then spiraling down the curving staircase and spinning into my room. In a round house, sound moves as the wind moves. Now it becomes visible when I look out the window and see how a breeze, as if released by her tune, has started whirling its way over and around the lilies and cosmos blooming in our yard. Soon the swaying oak and Douglas fir that shade the house in late afternoon lose themselves in her playing too. It seems to me that dance is rippling in one great loop through the breath of every living thing here. So there is only one thing for me to do. I stand and sing out the chorus.

Living in a house with no corners to send the waves careening, there is a sense of natural flow to everyday sounds. A resonance occurs, especially in one particular spot directly under the skylight, where the least whisper is amplified and can fill the whole living room. Setting a round house in isolation also seems to enhance silence, to give it palpable volume. Which in turn allows a sparrow's full song to come clear: *sweet zeet zeet zeee diddle diddle dee.* Beverly and I have become ridiculously sensitive to urban clangor, coming home from our trips to Portland feeling rattled and jangled.

Not only sound, but air circulates freely here too. That is why round houses are considered the best according to principles of Feng Shui. In her book *Feng Shui in 10 Simple Lessons*, Jane Butler-Biggs says, "to create a sense of tranquility, go for curving walls and corridors." Further, having the center space open to the sky, as ours is through its five-foot skylight, promotes inner stillness.

The circle implies wholeness, a perfect and never-ending containment. It also suggests an embrace, the encircling welcome or acceptance. Love, Thomas Aquinas said, works in a circle, and for us this has been the space where love flourished. Round buildings are thought to be geometrically stronger and more efficient than conventional rectangular or square designs, and physics recognizes the circle as the strongest shape. All these abstractions feel concrete to us in this house, tangible as the cedar exterior siding or fir joists holding the floor together. In *Black Elk Speaks*, the great Holy Man of the Oglala Sioux says, "the power of the world always works in circles, and everything tries to be round." That is the spirit that often seizes us here.

With curtainless windows in all directions, including up, we have a panoramic view and can sometimes feel genuine harmony with the elements. Well, we could if there were water to harmonize with. Or if we could see past the heavily leafing trees in summer, and did not have to cover the skylight with a sheet to shield us from the intensely focused beam of scorching summer sun, and if the landscape would only stop trying to move inside with us. Or if, in winter, the fog and clouds did not sock us in entirely and make it so that all we can harmonize with is darkness.

I have never been able to make sense of the relationship between our upstairs and downstairs rooms. The curving staircase, I think, throws me off. How can the bathroom be underneath our front porch when it seems to be all the way over on the opposite wall, just at the bottom of the stairs? How can my writing room have the same view as the window further west upstairs when it ought, I think, look out to the east since I have to go all the way over in that direction to get downstairs?

A few years ago in Parrott, Georgia, a man named Gary Buford had to move out of his house during a divorce. According to an Associated Press news feature, Buford was opposed to renting, so he decided to settle in a nice round corn bin on some farm property he owned. Once he got rid of the leftover, weevilly corn and paid for his one-dollar building permit, he proceeded to turn the twenty-seven foot wide, twenty-one foot high steel cylinder into very comfortable digs. His only complaint was that living in a round house requires some adjustments.

I know what he means. Coming as I do from Brooklyn, and having lived in a downtown Portland apartment building before joining Beverly in 1992, I was slow to adjust to life in the round. And as my spatial confusion suggests, I still have not finished adjusting. But it feels like home to me, and I know there is real truth to the saying used by Deltec Homes of Asheville, North Carolina, builders of round homes, who say, "You don't live in a square world . . . why live in a square home?"

We are moving to the Olympic Peninsula. To the northeast corner, up there by Puget Sound and the Strait of Juan de Fuca, a pocket of land shadowed by the Olympic Mountains and lying along the quiet inner shoreline of Washington state. Has everything we want. Mellow, predictable weather; abundant waters that are much calmer than the crashing Pacific of the Oregon coast; small pockets of community with lots of undeveloped space still available; great gardening conditions; close enough to Seattle or Victoria, British Columbia, to allow us an occasional urban fix.

A few years ago, we spent our anniversary on the peninsula, staying at a bed-and-breakfast near the base of Dungeness Spit. The nearest town was Sequim, pronounced Skwim, a retirement zone that brags about its mild winters and summers. After a hike on the spit and a round of croquet, we managed to browse a few neighborhoods and imagined ourselves living in the Dungeness Valley, maybe between lavender farms and elk pastures, with 306 days of temperate sunshine a year. This was an area we knew, an integral part of our relocation fantasia. Port Ludlow, Port Hadlock, and Paradise Bay to the south; we had drifted through them all during the last half decade, not exactly house hunting, but not simply touring either.

Now we reserve a cottage for a week on Discovery Bay. A very romantic setting nestled amidst trees overlooking one of scenic Discovery Bay's finest beaches, that is what the Web site tells us. Just the right spot for us to set up headquarters and scout for potential homes. Get a feel for the area. While also, of course, having our summer vacation along the sparkling clean waters and among the marine wildlife.

The drive takes more than five hours. That does seem excessive if we are to be visiting our parents in Portland. But wait, surely we could return once a month and stay overnight with Beverly's parents or sister, keep an eye on things. Or, we think, tired as we are after the drive, every two months.

We settle into our cottage on Discovery Bay and find the neighborhood overrun with vacationing families. There are cottages on both sides of us! Kids screaming, parents tense and rattling pots in cramped kitchens, pandemonium of motor boats on the water, and RVs on the road that runs behind the cottages. Every few minutes, small planes take off from an airport just over the trees beyond the road. So we do more scouting of real estate than we planned, but nothing we find feels quite right. The peninsula is too crowded for us; the people who write that the area is still wide open do not dwell in our kind of isolation. The places we like are too expensive. From the nice house near Dabob Bay we watch an enormous Trident submarine glide past the restricted beach. Bangor, the U.S. Naval Nuclear Submarine Station, is located nearby. Let your kayak get within a thousand yards of a Trident and it will sink you, we are told. From the porch of another house we watch the vacant lot that separates it from a small development being cleared by a bulldozer.

The drive home to Amity seems even longer than the drive to the peninsula, the reverse of our usual experience of time. Maybe we would have to visit our parents quarterly, not monthly.

It is so good to be home that we realize we can never move. If we need more space, we should just add on to the house. If we need to be by water, we should rent small places for a month by water. If we need to get away, we should get away. Then come home.

But when we think about adding on to our house—a wing jutting out to the east; a second, smaller circle connected by a short breezeway—we worry about disturbing the perfect circle we already have, or turning the area into a construction zone and disturbing the site. When we feel the urge to be by water, we pack up and leave with great enthusiasm. Then we come home earlier than planned. A five-day vacation in the San Juan Islands last month turned into a four-day vacation; three years ago, we stayed five days at a cottage we rented for a week on Washington's Long Beach peninsula.

I keep feeling that all this is something we should be able to sort out with logic. Make a chart, put STAY on one side and MOVE on the other, list advantages and disadvantages, and analyze the problem. Scientific method! Identify premise (we cannot live here anymore). Gather information (house too small, land too hard, water too scarce), formulate an hypothesis (move to larger house on more welcome land near water), deduce implications (sell old house, buy new house), and conclude (move). But facts are interconnected and mood changes and we cannot always assign value to competing desires and pretty soon we are lost in a kind of circular logic. We assume as a premise—that we have to move—the conclusion we seek. *Circulus in demonstrando.*

We have, I suppose, lived too long in our circular domicile. So long, that we have come to think in circles when we think of home. Or perhaps not long enough. Perhaps the circle is our mandala, our ritualistic, geometric meditative design, and we have not quite gone far enough with it to get our thinking straight.

In 1988, when Beverly bought this property, it was a ragged trapezoid of undeveloped land near the top of the Amity Hills, zoned for tree farming. There was evidence of logging earlier in the century, and of wildfire damage. A paved road led up the hill, left over from an earlier attempt at creating a subdivision.

She spent weekends camped on the land, coming out from her rented home in Portland to get a sense of where and how she wanted to build the house while causing the least site damage. Then she contracted with a company called Oregon

Yurtworks, designed the house with them, and in May, 1989, over the course of two long weekends and with the help of friends and family, the house shell was erected. She moved in four months later.

Beverly felt at home here even before the house was built. She had known for many years that she wanted to live in the woods; that she needed a small, isolated place for herself, bathed in silence and light, a space so open and flowing that it would bring a wholeness to her experience of home and nature.

I had not thought much about the idea of Home. I just wanted to be with Beverly. For me, to feel at home only seemed to require space for my writing desk and books, and the absence of outside disturbance. The rest was negotiable. I had lived in eighteen different urban dwellings before joining Beverly in rural Amity.

But I have lived here longer than anywhere now. If I have ever felt truly at home, it has been in this house on this land. Dry as it is, hard as it is, this place slakes some powerful thirst that I hardly recognize having. Thinking of such deep quenching brings to mind the final two lines of Robert Frost's poem, "Directive," which I have always loved. It is about a ruined house on a ruined farm in a ruined town, a site so worn down it would seem to offer no sustenance at all. Yet it touches something essential in the poet, who says, "Here are your waters and your watering place./Drink and be whole again beyond confusion."

Yet, like Beverly, I feel that my time here is nearing an end. That feeling, which emerges as a genuine but vague pressure and without my thinking about it, sparks the urge to move as much as anything so specific as water, rock, or room.

We are moving to Portland. We need to be in the city, where the water supply is famous for its quality, where we can attend readings and lectures and concerts and plays, where we can live in a new house in which everything works, where there are two rivers, and lakes are not far away. Be near the parents.

No, we are moving to the Portland suburbs. Still have the benefits of the city but at a more affordable price, and more space, and some greenery. But not in a development. Not close to traffic or clutter. So no, not Portland or the suburbs.

We are moving to another part of the county where we live now. That makes sense. More house for the money. Yamhill County is still rural and largely undiscovered. It is wine country, a richly rolling landscape with climate more like Sicily's than like the clichéd Pacific Northwest's. Maybe we can scale down our water requirements and settle near a pond.

We drive along Hidden Hills Road. What a suitable name! Our friend Lynne lives near the road's end and we are going to visit her to welcome the summer solstice. We come around a curve and pass a property we have seen before. Still for sale! Beverly slams on the brakes and we back up. Look at that: a large home on about two and a half acres of land drifting down toward a creek, a garage, a separate building that would work perfectly as a studio for Beverly.

Beverly grabs a flyer and the details are splendid. Why, the well is rated at eighty gallons a minute, ten times greater than the new well we drilled to replace the first one. Already we are divvying up the space—I will use an upstairs bedroom for my office, Beverly will paint and store her art in the outbuilding and play music in the bonus room, we will use the family room as a library, the hidden back deck with its view of pasture is perfect for her daily *qi gong* exercises.

A few days later, after returning from a trip to the San Juan Islands and deciding not to move there, we make an appointment with the realtor and look at the house on Hidden Hills Road.

It was not as advertised. Nothing usually is.

We are so happy to be home, we say we are finished looking elsewhere. Nothing is as good as what we have. And we believe that, we really do. Though we both know it will not be long before we are scouring real estate ads and browsing the Internet for new listings.

In 1968, when I was a student actor at Franklin & Marshall College, my roommate, Lou Hampton, and I drove from Lancaster, Pennsylvania, to New York City to see a production of *In Circles*, a play based on the writings of Gertrude Stein. It was a one-act musical, assembled by Al Carmines, that made use of Stein's *A Circular Play* and added other bits as well. A group of characters, ostensibly in a country house garden, sang lyrics about their states of mind, phrases that made little immediate sense but lingered. It was a play about circles of feeling, circles of relationship, circles of thought, that made use of suitably non-linear lyrics and was passionate in ways that defied explanation.

I bought the cast album and listened to it, took it with me to graduate school in Illinois after I had left acting and turned to writing, played it until the grooves wore out. When my daughter, Rebecca, was young, I sang the songs for her and she loved them, so I bought another copy of the album and we listened together for years.

One character says that a circle is a necessity. She believes that each of us has our essential circles. I know that Beverly and I have them, and our circles overlap often, which may be why we get along so well. They fit together within the circle of our house to create a complete sense of home. But circles can *include* as well as exclude, or, as Gertrude Stein says when claiming that a circle is a necessity: "Otherwise you would see no one." Beverly and I have both begun to admit a desire to see more people, to feel a closer connection to community. Maybe that is behind the increasing urgency we feel about moving from here. Also, maybe we need another kind of beauty. Circles are not the only source of rapture, after all, and "a great deal of beauty is rapture." Maybe we need a few years outside the perfection of this circle we live in, something with rougher edges to deal with. Or maybe we simply need a change, because home is a process as much as it is a place, and we are ready for the next step in the process.

Reading Gertrude Stein leads me to reading Robert Frost because I can only tolerate small doses of non-linearity. And reading Frost leads me to reading his dear friend Edward Thomas, the British poet who perished during World War I at the age of thirty-nine. In Thomas' relatively brief *Collected Poems*, there are three poems entitled "Home," three others with the word "House" in their titles, and several more that are about the idea of Home. In the last of his "Home" poems, Thomas describes the circularity represented by the way Beverly and I are thinking nowadays. He says that the land he thinks of as Home is, in truth, land he has never seen, a place he has never even heard of. If he could find it, he fears that "my happiness there,/Or my pain, might be dreams of return/Here, to these things that were."

As of now, we are not moving anywhere. Soon, the blooming blackberries—those relentless invaders we have battled for years—will be laden with fruit. I will walk up our gravel driveway to the road every morning and pick a colander full of ripe berries for our breakfast. We will sit at our round oak dining table and look out at the woods in full leaf shading us from the rising sun's intensity but blocking our view of the valley. I will gaze up at our skylight, covered till October by an old flannel sheet to protect us from the afternoon's blaze, and mention that we need to patch the hole that allows a small laser of heat through at the worst time of day. One or the other of us will probably pull out the map of Oregon and we will start talking about our next little scouting trip, disguised as a vacation.

We are staying here. But we are moving.

## 13  Turning Up the Gravity

Portland's Sunday evening news forecast rain for the valleys of western Oregon. But by 10:00, when Beverly and I went to bed, snow was falling. Thick flakes stuck to the grass, shrubs, and tree limbs.

We woke up at around 2:00 and could see the snow-cover even before Beverly turned on our outside light. The ground glowed. Our house is at an elevation of seven hundred feet, and though we seldom get snow up here, even in December, this time we were high enough to catch a storm that barely touched the valley floor. The old wooden chair on our deck had a good four inches nestled into its seat, maybe more.

At 3:34, a series of sharp cracks and flashes woke us again. After a few moments, we heard more cracks. The sounds seemed to be coming from everywhere at once, encircling the house.

"Did you hear that?" Beverly whispered.

"Thunder?" Then the room lit briefly with another flash. Its light seemed strange, tinting the hill's snow-covered landscape milky blue. "Thunder and lighting in December?"

I felt Beverly's head shake. "No, it's aliens," she mumbled. "You can tell by the color of the light. They're trying to find a place to land."

"They probably think our house is one of their long-lost ships."

She threw back the blanket and got out of bed.

"You don't have to go out and meet them," I said.

"I'd better fill the tub with water in case we lose power."

If we lose power, we lose our water supply too, because the well water is drawn by an electric pump and treated by an electric purification system. No flushing the toilet, no shower, no coffee or tea. I got up to find the jugs of drinking water we'd stored.

We went back to sleep until another series of cracks woke us again, at 4:47. This time they sounded more like rifle shots than thunder. We could hear a whoosh in the aftermath, and the thud of something heavy hitting the ground. There was more blue lightning too, vivid and bright, rinsing everything in a cold cobalt wash.

I knew it was 4:47 because I looked at my bedside digital clock just as its red face went blank. In the hall, the pale green glow from our bathroom nightlight vanished. The telephone jangled once, like a shutting shop door, and stopped.

"Power's gone," Beverly said.

That's when we realized that the cracking sounds we'd been hearing were large tree limbs breaking throughout the woods, and the thud was their impact against snow-packed ground. The blue lightning came from power lines sparking as they snapped and fell somewhere on the valley floor, probably near the spot where they head underground as our hill begins its rise a mile from here.

"I hope none of those limbs hits our car."

We listened some more. "Or the shed where the water storage tank is."

"We should call the power company and let them know."

"We should light a fire in the woodstove."

"All right," I said. Then we both fell asleep again.

I've lived here for eleven years and have never seen more than a few inches of snow accumulate. Most winters, there's barely a dusting, and temperatures seldom dip below freezing. If I want snow, I can go to the mountains, a ninety-minute drive east, where the snow pack is usually ten feet deep.

But I don't want snow. I had all the snow I want during the

thirteen years I lived in the Midwest. Avoiding snow was one of the main reasons I moved to western Oregon twenty years ago.

Several of my most visceral memories of those Midwest years are associated with snow and ice: my car, creeping on its new snow tires, sliding helplessly past the babysitter's house as I went to pick up my daughter after work; ice crusting my moustache and beard, frozen into a grimace after a four-mile run through a snowy park; shoveling the driveway shortly after midnight and again just before dawn during a blizzard, not being able to sleep as I tried to keep ahead of the accumulation; hearing the clank of loose tire chains as a salt truck drove along the street, or the deep hum of a city snow plow, its headlights revealing a chaos of whirling flakes; seeing mile after mile of white oak trees sheered off at their tops after an ice storm.

Earlier still I remember feeling ejected from time as my brother's small Ford Falcon began a slow, almost dainty, spin on an icy road on Long Island. The streetlights and house-lights and headlights from oncoming cars were all in the wrong places, and the asphalt glittered as we spiraled for hours through an intersection and slammed into an oncoming Buick. We'd moved in dream time, and it seemed that the inevitable crash took a week to happen. The moments before impact, the endless anticipation rather than the impact itself or the injuries that followed, remain precise and fixed in memory.

My only weather nightmares are about snow. From childhood, I remember living through Hurricane Donna, the fifth strongest ever recorded in the United States, which made landfall on the Long Island shore two days after my Bar Mitzvah in September 1960. *So this is what it means to be a man!* Dull red bricks were tossed all over the beachfront city of Long Beach, where I lived, landing in strange clusters on lawns or street corners. Wind ripped the boardwalk apart. Driftwood from the shore showed up here and there throughout downtown, a sodden sculptural installation. I walked along the beach during the hurricane's 100-mile-wide eye, shocked by the color and scent of the air. Long Beach, a narrow barrier island, was flooded from its ocean shore to its bay front. But I don't dream about hurricanes.

I don't dream about earthquakes, either, though I can't forget what it felt like when Beverly and I woke to find our house trembling one night in 1993. Nor do I dream about tornadoes, though I remember racing away from one, terrified, as I drove my daughter across the Illinois prairie in 1974 with no place to turn or hide.

No, it's snow that frightens me in the deepest, most irrational way. For this reason, I cannot watch the movie *Doctor Zhivago*. Maybe it's a genetic thing, something inherited from my Russian Jewish ancestors, who came from a place where men on horseback materialized out of the snow to murder them. I also hate to read about mountain expeditions that went wrong. The slow trudge across glaciers and encounters with crevasses and avalanches and tents routinely buried in snow. I identify totally with Gabriel Conroy and his slowly swooning soul as he hears snow "falling faintly through the universe" at the end of James Joyce's classic story, "The Dead." When I read John Greenleaf Whittier's poem, "Snow-Bound," I am desolate for him, probably more desolate than the perky poet himself, who is already making the best of things, seeing a fresh new beginning, when he writes, after two days of snow: "we looked upon a world unknown,/On nothing we could call our own." That sounds horrible to me.

In the morning, I went outside with a ruler and took measurements. The power might be gone, we might be snowed in for weeks without enough fresh fruit and vegetables, but at least I would have data!

On the small, grassy shelf of flat land between our house and the hill's crest, the snow was fourteen inches deep. It spread thickly over the humped forms of lavender, spirea, and fern. A drift by the deck was eighteen and a half inches deep, its edge curled up toward the clouds in a kind of pompadour.

Beverly's delicate Japanese maple curtseyed under the snow's weight, only three inches of its tip visible and tilted shyly down, wearing a white crown. Nearby, a slender madrone, twenty feet tall, that we'd transplanted seven years ago and placed where we could watch its growth from our bedroom window, had collapsed over the edge of the hill, roots once again visible. Our gazebo-shaped bird feeder wore a ten-inch top hat.

Moving west, I found that I could no longer pass beneath the laden branches of fir sagging near our front door. The fence around our vegetable garden had folded in on itself under the snow's pressure. Beside the storage shed, an oak limb, twisted like a corpse in *rigor mortis,* lay two feet behind our car, a near-miss. The limb was twelve feet long and half a foot thick.

I walked up the path toward the road, about two hundred yards from our house, tossing aside branches as I went, relieved that none of the trees looming over our gravel driveway had fallen. A few groaned, reminding me to be thankful there was little wind for them to bear.

"You know what they call those big limbs?" Beverly called after me. "Widowmakers. Be careful."

When I came around a curve in our driveway, I saw two large fir fallen where the driveway meets the road, blocking access. They had taken down the mailbox and newspaper tube, and just missed the telephone cable box. When I reached them, I saw that two more fir had fallen completely across the road as well. I didn't need my ruler to know that Beverly and I had a full morning's work with a chainsaw ahead of us.

Despite the stillness and quiet, the scene registered as aggressive, distorted. There was silence, but it was a foreboding silence, not peaceful at all. Everywhere I looked, trees and wild blackberry vines were misshapen by a thick layer of wet snow. It looked as though more trees would fall and that snow slides would result from the blows. The sky was a shade of gray that suggested stain rather than color, with no hint of the reflected, white sky glow known as snowblink.

Looking along our narrow road to where it met the main road leading down off the hill, I saw that all the familiar contours had been obliterated. The valley was gone. The foothills of the Coastal Range were gone. White ground merged with low clouds, and the view felt ruthlessly compacted. Swirled snow had settled in a series of chaotic, overlapping waves. It seemed a visual equivalent of white noise, disturbing the regular music of my visual surroundings. The obliterated landscape reminded me of the eradicated expressions on faces at the nursing home's Memory Impairment Unit.

My way of seeing, my vision, felt compromised, and what I saw seemed truly "a world unknown," revealing nothing I recognized as my own. An alien landscape. Made worse by the fact that my winters here have been mild, that I'd never seen the Amity Hills like this before.

Though I'd witnessed far worse snowstorms in the Midwest, though this scene was bound to be only a short-term inconvenience and could easily have been perceived as beautiful, though I recognized my response as excessive, I felt tense and dejected. *Buck up!* I told myself. *Think Jack London! Think Shackleton!*

By the time I walked back to the house, Beverly, who is as sensible about snow as I am deranged, had worked out a plan. For the rest of the morning, we sawed the four fallen fir into six or eight segments and dragged them to the margin of the woods. We righted the mailbox and newspaper tube, and hammered them into place. Ten strokes of the hammer. We swept clear the steps leading into the house. We examined the condition of trees near our house and determined exactly where to situate the car to reduce its risk of getting clobbered by a widowmaker. We carried a dozen logs from the woodpile into the house. Then we sat in the living room, too hot to need a fire, still sweaty and filthy, unable to wash ourselves, and ate almond butter sandwiches off paper plates for lunch.

I called the power company again and learned that I was the ninety-third person from my service area to report the outage.

They were aware of the problem and could not estimate when power would be restored. Beverly and I picked up our books and settled in.

Whittier's poem "Snow-Bound" is over nine hundred lines long. It was published in 1866 and sold over twenty thousand copies, a truly popular and enduring American work, and I felt that reading it as we waited for power to be restored would be a good, healthy thing for me to do. Better than watching for signs of snow melting, which was what I did for the first twenty minutes after lunch. Get some perspective on this little storm of ours, since Whittier's was one of those two-day New England doozies, a December blizzard remembered from his boyhood, full of the "swarm/ And whirl-dance of the blinding storm." Early on the poem has lots of venerable and apt adjectives like "cheerless," "ominous," "hoary," "dreary," "mindless," and "savage," that played right into my mood. But then it becomes an extended paean to the comforts of family togetherness and storytelling around the hearth: "What matter how the north-wind raved?/Blow high, blow low, not all its snow/Could quench our hearth-fire's ruddy glow." Humbug!

So I turned to Ralph Waldo Emerson's poem from 1846, "The Snow-Storm," still seeking a kindred spirit. But Mr. Self-Reliance was no help, coming as he does in the poem to admire "the mad wind's night-work,/The frolic architecture of the snow."

Soon I lost myself in the quest for a suitably despondent snow poem. But I kept finding poems full of the hooey of snowy beauty. Howard Nemerov has a poem celebrating the snowflake "perfected in the moment of its fall" and May Sarton, in "Snow Light," finds delight with her lover for a while "In the swan light,/In the white-on-white light/Of a winter storm." In "sno," e. e. cummings likes "the white idea" and talks about snowflakes in his cutest manner: "tiny, angels sharpen: themselves." For Gary Snyder in "The Snow on Saddle Mountain," snow is seen as "the only thing that can be relied on" and "the only faint source of hope." For Charles Wright, in "Snow," swirling flakes suggest the biblical human dust rising and re-congregating in the wind after death, then falling back to earth, an image of regeneration and hope. Robert Bly loves the "privacy" of a snowy night in "Driving to Town Late to Mail a Letter" and for Philip Levine, the snow that "has been falling for hours" on Detroit is "more beautiful than even the spring/grass which once unfurled here/before the invention of steel and fire." Capping their post-coital delight, the lovers in Frederick Morgan's "Winter Poem" breathe in air "washed clean by snow." In "Snow," an early work by the Irish poet Louis MacNeice, the speaker is much taken by a contrast between snow and pink roses as they rest together against his window. It delights him: "World is suddener than we fancy it," he says, thrilled by the image before his eyes. "World is crazier and more of it than we think,/ Incorrigibly plural." What is it with all these poets?

At least Wallace Stevens, in "The Snow Man," recognizes that snow—for any but those most used to winter and cold—can bring with it the feeling of "misery in the sound of the wind" and the suggestion of nothingness, "the nothing that is not there and the nothing that is." And Robert Frost, in "Desert Places," identifies with the loneliness of a snowy field where "all animals are smothered in the lairs." "Lonely as it is," he says, "that loneliness/Will be more lonely ere it will be less."

But the snow didn't make me feel lonely. Cut off, maybe, trapped, but not lonely, since I was with Beverly, together all day as normal. I was more in harmony with those animals smothered in the lairs, myself, and with that view of snow as a blanker whiteness expressing An Endless Nothing.

I was, it became clear, feeling threatened, despite the reliable protection of our house, plenty of supplies left over from our Y2K preparations, a functioning telephone, and the high likelihood of restored power by day's end.

In fact, according to literature I've gotten off the Internet, we were extraordinarily well-prepared for a snow emergency. We were Winter Wise! We were adequately insured and our documents were stored in a safe. Our supplies at home and in the car were in handy locations: first aid kits and essential medicines CHECK. Packaged, dried and canned foods CHECK. Non-electric can opener CHECK. Portable radio CHECK. Drinking water in closed, clean containers CHECK. We even had tap water stored to use in flushing the toilet while our power was gone. Car was fueled and we had some cash on hand. We also had extra batteries in all sizes, candles and matches, flashlights, lanterns that run on lamp oil and lanterns that run on batteries. We had lamp oil and we had extra wicks. We even had kitty litter, for times when our two cats couldn't bring themselves to go outside.

I tried not to spend too much time standing at our living room windows waiting for signs that things were improving. The thick snowy cloak reminded me that a glacial sheet had long ago covered this landscape, and its retreat had created the hill we live upon. The view reminded me of a passage in Verlyn Klinkenborg's book, *The Rural Life*, where he describes an upstate New York December snow: "it looked as though someone had turned up the planet's gravity during the night." Everything I saw was, like my mood, weighted down, hunched. Grave. Even the gray squirrels, flocking to the bird feeders, appeared burdened. They skittered on the snow, barking, their side-by-side diamond-shaped tracks elongated by the strange footing.

At 4:00, the phone rang. It was the power company's automated system informing us that our power had been restored. We called back and spent a half hour making it clear that our power had not been restored, and were put on the list of outages once again. We called every few minutes to check on the new estimated time of restoration.

As night fell, we lit candles and lanterns, stoked up the fire in the wood stove, and settled into our chairs, squinting, to read some more. Candle and lantern light are warmer, dimmer, and smellier than electric light, suitably drearier than what we were accustomed to. We were resigning ourselves to going to sleep without showers when, shortly after 6:00, the power came on. I raced around the house resetting clocks and urging the water heater to get down to business. The phone rang.

We thought the return of our power was the beginning of the end. But then we turned on the television and heard the weather forecast which, unfortunately, was correct this time. The beginning was just beginning.

It snowed off and on for the next five days, across the old year's end and the new year's start. Then there was a brief weekend dry spell, with temperatures reaching the upper thirties, followed by three full days of sleet and freezing rain. A two-inch crust of ice topped the remaining foot of snow, turning the land into a pocked and glistening moonscape, sealing the car, glazing every surface. It's easy to overlook how uneven the land is, inch by inch, until it ices over and you try to maintain balance. We stayed indoors, got no mail, no UPS deliveries. Icicles dangling from our roof became another object that I could study for signs of change, checking throughout the days for the first drips that would indicate thawing.

When the thawing finally came, Beverly and I had been snowbound for twelve out of thirteen days. Several times every day, as we kept ourselves busy around the house, the phone would ring once and, when I picked it up, the line would be dead. I'd hang up, then lift the receiver and hear no dial tone. Then I'd march around the house, picking up other extensions, each of them dead. Going back to the phone that rang, I'd kneel, unplug the wall jack and plug it back in, lift the receiver and listen. If there was still no dial tone, I'd go from phone to phone, six in all, disconnecting and reconnecting each in sequence to see if that brought things back to life. Eventually, a dial tone would arise, but we could never detect any pattern: Start downstairs? Start upstairs? Start downstairs, but only if the phone that had rung to tell us the line was dead was an upstairs phone? One time, it was the upstairs cordless phone that came back to life after we reconnected it twice; next time, it was the cordless in the bedroom on the third try and the time after that it was the land-line phone beside Beverly's recliner, but only after we'd said an elaborate prayer. Once it was disconnecting and reconnecting the fax machine that triggered a return of the dial tone.

The resolution was obviously random, and it had nothing to do with our unplugging/replugging activities. Sometimes, when we'd be talking on the phone, the line would crackle and we could hear the faint sound of someone dialing or the distant sound of a voice buzzing. Other times, static was deafening, like an aural equivalent to our ongoing snowstorms. But worst of all was the spontaneous ringing followed by a blanketing, deathly silence, which in turn meant a parade through the house to tinker with phone jacks. The whole thing seemed an unnerving, almost taunting gesture on the part of our only remaining viable connection to the outside world.

It took two full weeks of this before I realized that I needed to call the phone company. That shows how dulled I'd become in the throes of confinement, and how my mind only started to work once the snow started to melt. The phone's problem, apparently, was a cable soaked or otherwise damaged by the storm. When they had it fixed, Verizon notified us by an automatic phone call.

The storms and their aftermath had become an erasure of the ordinary. All the familiar views were effaced. My sense of linkage to the community below, the way we watched weather and time move in the valley and on the hills opposite, the way horses neighing or cattle lowing kept us in touch with our neighbors' farms on the flatlands, was disturbed. Time itself was restructured as the usual markers of a day's passage became suspended. Along with the phone, Internet service became unpredictable, and occasionally e-mails weren't reaching their destinations. Our regular routine was reorganized around snow-related tasks, land and house maintenance, heat and water provision. I discovered how much the quotidian means to me, and how lost I feel when the customary, normally unremarked elements of daily life disappeared.

With nowhere to go, I went inward. I felt the loss of balance and traction as internal phenomena, not just external ones, and realized that this freak storm, unprecedented in all my time here, was forcing me to confront certain fundamental things about myself. For instance, I still have work to do in facing my fears of entrapment. I know they stem from the times my mother locked me in my toy chest or cornered me behind an open door to hold me in place as she kicked and punched. They also relate to my sense of being trapped by illness, even now, as the storm arrived shortly after the fifteenth anniversary of the day I got sick. I remain disabled, sharply limited in how freely I can walk or how much work I can achieve. The unexpected encounter with erasure that this snowstorm provided also rekindled my fears of dementia and death. Of being silenced. Which is exactly what the virus that attacked me seemed to intend, scarring my brain with lesions, compromising my memory and concentration and abstract reasoning powers. The storm was also a showdown with disorder, and with the implacable power of natural forces, the strangeness of waking to December thunder and blue lightning. On the other hand, perhaps I was simply being a nervous idiot who should stop fretting and enjoy the beauty, enjoy the break, go out and throw snowballs at the squirrels who were making it impossible for birds to use the feeders.

I knew that my reaction to the storm involved all of these things combined. While conditions remained as they were, thirteen days that seemed to have slipped out of time became a perfect occasion for obsession. The thing I had to do was write about the experience, to refuse the silence. And I began walking our hill as soon as the melting began. As the snow disappeared, it left bizarre formations on the road's edge, blackened by dirt, that looked like sculptures by Jean Dubuffet. The sawn limbs we'd dragged to the wood's margins were actually resting in ditches and hanging out into the road. It seemed as though the normal disorder within the woods had moved out now to the cleared spaces—the road, driveway, yard—reasserting its claim over our efforts at civilization. A fifteen foot long oak bough pierced the woodshed's makeshift fiberglass roof like a spear and stuck in the mud. Soon, like the generations of rural dwellers before us, we would have to begin the spring cleanup.

# 14  A Stable State

After breakfast, I place my mug of leftover coffee in the bread-box, shut the door and turn its knob. Then I walk over to the living room windows.

As always, these next ninety seconds, while my coffee re-heats, are a splendid time to watch birds a the feeder. An evening grosbeak! No, too small; it's a goldfinch. Then there's a wren-sparrow-robin. It's chased off by a Stellar's jay, the big blue loudmouth with a pointy crest that I never have trouble identifying. I'm from Brooklyn, New York, and though I've lived in these woods for more than a decade now. am slow to learn my birds.

Five minutes pass before I realize I must have missed the microwave's signal. I walk back and open its door. The coffee is gone. Did I press the wrong button and vaporize the mug? I remember putting it somewhere that had a door. It's not in the refrigerator. Not in the oven or pantry. It's not in the garbage. By the time I locate my mug inside the breadbox, I've lost all desire for reheated coffee.

Since morning is my best time, mistaking the breadbox for the microwave before 9:00 a.m. alarms me a little. I've been do-ing fairly well for the past few months and the last thing I need is a relapse of my neurological symptoms. Nearly fifteen years after getting sick, I've learned how to maintain my health at a modest level of equilibrium. But it's a volatile equilibrium. As long as I don't get overtired, as long as I don't contract some kind of infection or other challenge to my already-compro-mised immune system, eat right, and control my expectations for walking or writing. I can function well for an hour or two every morning. I can say "out the window" instead of "at the elbow" when describing where I watch birds. I can use my key rather than a pen when trying to lock the front door of the house, can pick up a spoon rather than a glass of water when I intend to stir the simmering kale, find the way to my writing room without forgetting why I'm going there, track the movement of clouds without falling over. Minor achievements, I know. But each one is a triumph of homeostasis, and taken together they permit the illusion of sound health. A stable state.

But I know that the stable state is as shatterable as glass. Brain damage has cut across most of my body's systems: overheating can lead to a week in bed, a cold can trigger months of neurological static, watching a tense movie can produce protracted fevers. When things are in balance, as they have been for months now, I feel graced by memory and by thought as they function with greater cohesion. Just last week, I was able to figure out how to operate the ratcheting clasp of a nylon cargo strap, a task requiring greater powers of abstract reasoning, memory, and physical dexterity than I can routinely command. The achievement left me giddy with pleasure.

When I'm in a stable state, I feel full of clarity in a way that I no longer take for granted because I have felt the emptiness of a blank mind, sometimes for months at a time. I have sprayed wasp-killer in my face, tried to cut my desk instead of the newspaper with my blue-handled scissors, said "crash the floor" when I meant to say "close the door." Intending to find a pair of jeans in my closet, I've folded back the sheets on our bed and felt baffled that my clothes were missing. I've wandered the woods around our house, utterly lost as soon as the rooftop vanished from sight, though I've walked those woods for more than a decade.

When memory and reason fail, when thoughts cannot cohere and time falls apart, I become trapped in a blizzard of fragmented images. A crazed, whirling storm of confusion, a kaleidoscopic cognitive white-out. Like a blind person who has lost all sense of visual cohesion, I forget what it's like to remember.

I want to avoid feeling that way again. This episode with the missing coffee mug could be an early sign of trouble; I might be slipping. But I don't perceive that clearly, which could be another sign. I blame the August heat.

The next morning, again in connection with my coffee preparations, I pour a full carafe of water into the filter basket rather than the coffee maker's water container. I don't even stop when the water begins cascading over the counter top. After sopping up the mess, I put the wet cloth in the freezer instead of taking it downstairs to the laundry room. I find it stiff and crusted with ice later that day, while looking in the freezer for a copy of the *New Yorker*.

Early afternoon, when the phone rings, I slip on my head-set and say, *Hello*, but the phone just keeps ringing. I speak louder, enunciating clearly so the caller will hear me, but the ringing continues and no one answers me. So I remove the headset and turn it around, placing the earpiece on my right side this time. Still no one answers. With the headset on and the phone ringing away, I walk out of the house to see if the reception might improve. Only when the answering machine picks up the call does the ringing stop, but the caller doesn't leave a message. Typical prank. Then it occurs to me that I'd neglected to press the headset's On button.

Evidence is beginning to mount. But when my symptoms flare, the powers of reason I might use to identify them have become compromised. I become too muzzy-headed to understand what's happening, to piece things together. Moment to moment experience remains vivid but fragmentary; I can't see its patterns.

That afternoon, when Beverly calls from her office and I actually manage to answer the phone, I explain what happened: "The prune was empty," I tell her. Even as I say that, instead of what I meant to say (something like *the phone rang, but no one was there*), I know it's wrong. But it is an intriguing way to describe the earlier phone fiasco, and I recognize it as one of my more memorable paraphasias. For good measure, I add, "Nothing there." *The prune was empty*, all right.

After eleven years together, Beverly is attuned to the flare-ups of my symptoms. She often knows what's happening to me before I do. Rather than ask what I meant by "the prune was empty," she says, "You must be tired."

I think *she's always so perceptive*. But instead of speaking, I shrug my shoulders.

"How do you feel?" she asks.

"Fine. Except for this fire on my inner elbow."

"Fire on your elbow?"

"I mean hive. I have a hive on my inner elbow." I look at it as I speak. Right there at the joint, winking at me. A little too blistery and full of fluid to be a typical hive, and an angrier red at the base than most hives, but it certainly itches like a hive. "Must've been something I ate."

"One hive?"

I nod. "On my kneebow."

By the time Beverly gets home that evening, I've noticed several more hives on my arms and neck, and can feel others across my back. But my breathing remains fine, and there are no other signs of allergic reaction.

We sit at the dining room table together, and she touches a few of them. "You know what that looks like?" she asks.

I nod, but say, "No. No way."

She goes and gets the books. *The Merck Manual of Medical Information* talks about crops of blebs, which sounds like something made up by Mel Brooks. But *The American Medical Association Family Medical Guide* has a photograph. A very gruesome photograph. A bumper crop of blebs.

I glance at Beverly's eyes, back at my hives, back at her eyes. It's a hot August night, summer's molten heart. "Prickly heat?" I say in the rising tones of false hope. I'm beginning to realize why I felt so strange all week.

Beverly raises her eyebrows. She turns the book around to show me the photograph. That sure is what I look like.

"Couldn't be," I say. "I'm fifty-five years old."

Chicken pox is a disease of childhood caused by the varicella-zoster virus. It's spread by airborne droplets and because chicken pox is so common among children, and because one attack confers lifelong immunity, nine out of ten adults in the United States are immune to it. Not me. Measles at four, German measles and mumps just before turning seventeen, catching both in the same grim May of 1964, but not chicken pox.

Beverly and I study our medical books. Descriptions of chicken pox in adults are alarming. According to *The Merck Manual of Medical Information*, which is beginning to irritate me, "the infection may be severe or even fatal in adults and especially in people with an impaired immune system." I'm adult; I have an impaired immune system. Under "Complications," there is a final encouraging note: "brain infection (encephalitis), which may occur toward the end of the illness or 1 to 2 weeks after, affects less than 1 in 1,000 cases" and "although the encephalitis may be fatal, the chances for complete recovery are generally good."

My system has already shown a penchant for allowing viruses to reach the brain. I close the book and realize that I must not be thinking clearly. I've taken a few isolated facts about chicken pox, mixed them together with my medical history and preexisting viral-induced brain damage, and concluded that it's time to get all my personal papers in order.

Then I think, "Hell, we don't even know if I have chicken pox." I must have said that out loud, because Beverly leans over and whispers, "We know you have chicken pox."

I look at her and nod. Then we call the clinic and tell them we're coming in.

For twelve hours, my case seems mild. A few itchy spots, no fever, none of that deeply rooted feeling of being sick to the core, a pocked apple that splits to reveal runaway rot. This is plausible. My doctor long ago described the state of my immune system as *erratic*. Parts of it fail to function, other parts fail to stop functioning. It's simultaneously stalled and in overdrive. I seldom catch colds, but when I do, the results are exaggerated and I'm sick for three months instead of three days. So at the outset, we can believe that the hyperactive part of my immune system is subduing the varicella-zoster virus.

I sleep through the night, and when I wake, a phrase keeps going through my mind: "a disease of childhood." Maybe catching chicken pox at fifty-five is actually a message: Grow up! Stop writing about your mother already! No, no, I know illness is not a metaphor. I have read my Susan Sontag. This has nothing to do with being haunted by the taints of childhood. This is a virus. But still, I can't help feeling somehow *responsible* for contracting this childhood sickness. What next, a passion for pabulum?

Immunologically speaking, diseases of childhood—provided we survive them—help the body construct a healthy system of defenses. As Nietzsche said, "that which does not kill us makes us stronger." The immune system builds its protection against specific disease-causing organisms only by encountering, identifying, and defeating them. We are not born immune to infections; we acquire immunity as part of the process by which we survive infections.

Childhood infections such as diphtheria, whooping cough, or polio were routinely fatal until medical science learned to induce immunity by immunization. But the other ubiquitous infections, often mild when encountered in childhood, can be devastating in later life, perhaps because by adulthood the immune system's capacity has become overloaded by a lifetime of other challenges.

As the first day progresses, proliferating blisters begin colonizing my torso, arms, and legs. I feel their spread as a flaming tautness across my face and back. A Crop of Blebs! A Storm of Vesicles! I get them in my mouth, ears, nose, throat. On my eyelids. My, um, organs of elimination and procreation. By mid-morning Saturday, the second day after onset, I am in the hospital emergency room, where the admissions specialist rattles off a sequence of horror stories about adults she has known who came down with chicken pox.

I am sick for two months. By mid-October, though my face and torso still show pox scars, I feel recovered. Actually, "recovered" doesn't do justice to what is happening. I feel terrific. Strong, clear in the head, capable of focusing. I write a check, correctly record the amount, subtract to get a new balance, and my calculator confirms that I've done it all correctly. A minor miracle. I open the refrigerator and, lo and behold, the newspaper is not in there, but the apple I'm looking for is! I feel better than I've felt in five or six years, which was the last time I'd been able to walk a mile, so I go out with Beverly to walk for twenty minutes. I even try walking for short periods without a cane, something I haven't done since early 1989.

It's bizarre, as though the bout of chicken pox has somehow reset my immune system, reorganized my chemical poise, and stabilized me at a level higher than I'd been at in years. As though, jolted by the invasion of varicella-zoster virus, my defenses became less scattered and erratic, pulled together by the challenge.

The healing process remains essentially mysterious. It is, to some, a kind of warfare in which invaders (viruses, bacteria, toxins) must be defeated by the combination of bodily defenses and medical reinforcements (drugs, surgery). To others, healing is the exact opposite of warfare, a reestablishment of harmony between body and spirit, or body and environment. It's about restoring the body's relationship to the vital energy of the universe. Some approach healing by seeking to suppress symptoms, attacking the apparent cause, while others approach it by working with the symptoms rather than against them, supplementing the body's effort to heal itself. Still others approach healing by trying to correct their attitudes or their way of life, or by prayer, by pilgrimage, appeasement. Or by a combination of all these approaches.

Me? All of the above, plus writing. I have spent fifteen years chronicling the ebb and flow of relapse and remission, the juncture where healing and managing illness meet. Now, in the ethereal zone of this sudden, pox-induced remission, I decide that the time has come to stop writing about illness. Telling this enigmatic story has brought me to a kind of clarity: having written about getting sick and finding my way back toward a stable state, having dealt with the ongoing fluctuations that make my stable state so volatile, my task must be to get on to other things. Not to focus on the minute adjustments or variations in my day-to-day health, or on the isolation that illness produces, but on what I encounter out there in the world. On the community and the flow of life from which I so easily become disconnected. Otherwise, obsessed with illness, I remain its hostage.

Like the virus that seems to have set me straight for a while, the world outside works its mysteries on me too. I have ignored that for too long, caught in the timeless stasis of chronic illness. Writing about life outside should be my next work, and this essay should be my Farewell to Illness.

Beverly and I drive down the hill to take a walk in "downtown" Amity, the small village located two miles from our house. I can walk a mile again, provided I walk on the flat land below rather than the hillside where we live. At Third and Trade streets, we see a Model A Ford waiting to turn left. It's a Hiboy two-door from the Hoover years, gray as the hair and old corduroy cap the driver sports. He wears thick goggles that sparkle in the sun, a bushy mustache, and a gleaming smile. It's as though he's emerged intact from a 1931 motor company advertisement. A Nash the color of glazed brick pulls up behind him and toots its horn, the driver waving a gloved hand. The Nash is joined by a four-door Hupmobile and a Dodge touring car driven by a man who looks asleep behind the wheel. In the passenger seat, a woman is all but hidden behind a floppy turquoise hat. They are all waiting for a Packard sedan to turn right, but the Packard is waiting for us to cross Trade Street and we are waiting to see what else emerges from the sun's glare. Another vintage car? Theodore Roosevelt?

Here we are, all frozen in time, the noon light like a gloss laid over what we've chosen to do with a Sunday morning, watching a past that none of us knew in person assemble itself before our eyes. From somewhere, perhaps a CD player hidden inside one of the cars, perhaps from a fold in the ether, we hear the strains of Hoagy Carmichael's "Star Dust," and take that as a signal that it's time to cross the street. If we stay where we are, pretty soon we'll have to start dancing the Charleston.

In the small village park across from the cemetery, more than a hundred cars are crammed together. Beverly and I stroll among the drivers, finding ourselves caught up in the spirit of passionate play. The cars are organized by era, and while we are intrigued with the lovingly restored cars from early in the twentieth century, it's the cars from the 1950s and early 1960s—our years of childhood and adolescence—that keep attracting us. A '61 Mercury Comet, like the one Beverly's family owned, which was wrecked because Fritzi, the dachshund, got himself wedged under her mother's feet. An Edsel, like the one owned by my driver's ed teacher during the summer of 1964, which had its automatic gear shift buttons located in the center of the steering wheel; a black '52 Buick, like the one my father drove through Brooklyn summer streets with the windows shut and the interior radiating heat; a '57 Chevy Impala I remember my brother coveting. Beverly and I walked around the park for most of an hour, smiling, telling each other stories evoked by the cars we passed.

Back home, I begin an essay about the year 1957. What was going on around me during that pivotal year in my life, when I was ten and everything I knew began to change.

The essay came quickly, which is unusual for me. Then I wrote an essay about the cities and villages where my four immigrant grandparents came from, and an essay about Achill Island, off the west coast of Ireland, where Beverly and I spent the summer of 1994. The outward-looking focus of this new work, each essay now a chapter of this book, seemed evident. I felt myself heading in a new and promising direction.

Then I had another relapse. Not apparently triggered by

something outside, a cold or an exposure to some allergen, and not by becoming overtired or stressed because I was taking care to avoid just such hazards. No. I don't know why my health fell apart again, or remained compromised for another six months. But I do know that *I'm rot slowing to night around it.* I mean, *I'm not going to write about it.*

## 15 Taking Stock

"What's your name, Mister?" my mother says to me. I am leaning across her body, buckling her into the car's passenger seat.

"I'm Floyd." The clasp finally clicks into place. "I'm your son."

"My son?" She smiles and closes her eyes. "Imagine that."

As I straighten up to close the door, her eyes fly open. "And who are you?"

I kiss her and say my name, then walk around the car and get in beside her. From the back seat, Beverly leans forward to adjust the shoulder strap. My mother has begun to sing: *Three blind mice, three blind mice.*

Her voluntary song repertoire has shrunk now to Mother Goose nursery rhymes. Prompted, she can still find a few snatches of old standards and tunes from Broadway shows, but on her own, the selections are all from earliest childhood.

"How are you doing, Mother?"

She nods at me but keeps on singing: *See how they run? See how they run?*

We are taking her to the doctor. My mother has a skin cancer lesion on her shoulder that needs to be removed because it's open and irritating her. The clinic is about a half hour's drive across Portland from the nursing home and we've allowed ourselves plenty of time to get her there. But it took almost fifteen minutes to walk from her room to the car and I'm beginning to feel a little rushed.

"Where are we going?"

"For a drive, Mother. Isn't it a beautiful day?"

"Where?"

I point toward the road ahead. "Out there."

"But how long till we get there?"

I can't help myself, caught up in the Abbott and Costello energy: "Where?"

She points toward the road ahead.

"Soon."

To which my mother says, no longer in the form of song but as sharply spoken dialogue, like a warning, and with her finger pointed toward me: "She cut off their TAILS with a CARVING KNIFE."

I realize that my attention is in several places at once. I'm listening to my mother, aware of how strange it must be for her to be away from the safety of the nursing home, in a car driven by someone she does not know, headed someplace she cannot imagine, hearing talk that she cannot follow, as a woman she cannot see places a comforting hand on her shoulder. I'm trying to ease her anxiety about where she's going by calling her attention to other things, as I did almost thirty years ago when driving my daughter to the doctor. I'm watching the traffic and the clock. And I cannot stop thinking about the moment we arrived at my mother's side today, in the solarium where she spends most of her time. Sitting alone at a table, she was gazing toward the wall as though mesmerized by a view only she could see. Her nearest companion was the elderly man at an adjacent table, a former dentist, bent over the prostrate body of a teddy bear and pantomiming an intricate procedure on its mouth. When we greeted my mother, and tried to explain who we were, she looked at the dentist and barked, "Why didn't you tell me they were coming!"

Like the shattered surface of a turbulent lake, my mother's mind is a meaningless dazzle of refractions and glimmers, winks of consciousness, cognitive chop. Occasionally, her old and true spirit flickers to the surface, as in her sharp reprimand of the dentist. But her mind can neither be still nor organize itself, and there is no let-up from the chaos. Nothing coheres; nothing is stable.

By the time we get off the elevator and enter the clinic,

we're late and my mother is very tired from all the unaccustomed walking. She stops in the hallway while Beverly consoles her. My mother's anxiety has been mounting, her voice rising, trembling. Still in place fifty-six years after its original installation, my internal seismic mother-o-meter registers signs of her imminent eruption. *Red Zone!* I hold the clinic door open with one hand and keep the other on my mother's arm. Once we're inside, I rush toward the receptionist's window and hear my mother cry at Beverly: "I want to go to my room."

The receptionist agrees that we should get into the examination room quickly. We're met there by a nurse, still in her twenties, whose voice is much too loud for the tiny space we share.

"Hop up onto the table, Lillian!"

My mother shudders and says, "What table?"

To which I add the idiotic observation: "She doesn't hop much anymore," then bend and with Beverly's help hoist my mother onto the table. We try to ease her into a supine position, thinking she might be calmer that way. But she struggles against us, flails, grabs my hair, and screams, *No no no no.* So we crank up the back of the table instead, and she sits perched on its edge, feet dangling. Her frown dissolves. She looks up at the bright lights.

Beverly and I each hold one of her hands and whisper to her. "Good job. Are you comfortable?"

She whispers back: "But what are you doing to me?"

"It's all right, Mother. The nurse just needs to check you over."

"What nurse?"

"Here, Lillian." The nurse slips a blood pressure cuff onto my mother's arm and tightens it.

"HELP!"

I'm not surprised that her levels are elevated. So is her pulse. She is rubbing her biceps and running her tongue over her lips. The nurse, as though propelled by one long sigh, moves toward the door.

"Doctor will be in soon."

"Please," I say. "You see what's happening here. Can you get him to come right away?"

She refuses to look back at me. "I'm afraid he's not in the office yet. Must be tied up somewhere in the hospital."

"No no no no." I sound just like my mother now.

The nurse opens the door, still looking away from me. But she says, "I'll page him," and points her pager at us like a stun-gun.

Then the door closes. My mother kicks her feet in tempo against the table and hums. *Did you ever see such a sight in your life?* Beverly and I look at each other and know, without speaking, what we have to do.

We sing songs from *Fiddler on the Roof.* Whenever we stop to recall another song, my mother fills the silence with "Three Blind Mice." We finish all we can remember from *Fiddler* and move on to *The King and I* as the door flies open and the doctor enters like the King on cue. I've never been happier to see a doctor in my life.

When he says, "Why don't you two wait outside now?" I have to restrain myself from giving him a kiss.

The doctor opens the waiting room door about ten minutes later. He's beaming and chuckling as he beckons us inside.

"Your mother," he said. "I just love that lady."

As he leans back against the wall, I hear him humming, *Three blind mice.* He's a burly man with thick black hair and a beard, and I know what my mother would have said about him a decade ago: *Looks like a Cossack!*

He straightens up and says the surgery was simple. His cupped hand moves through the air between us. "Scooped it right out, no problem."

But he won't meet my eye. I know he's telling me that my mother's skin cancers are not going to kill her, that there's no real point in concerning ourselves with them. Only with her comfort. We had a similar discussion, by phone, almost two years ago, when he first talked to me about her newly detected breast cancer. I believe he hopes I'm not going to question him now about her malignancies, that I understand he can't tell me whether they're spreading or how long she has left to live. Still symptom-free, her body remains in a vague state of suspension not unlike the pestilential state of her consciousness, riddled with corruption, eaten away, slipping irreparably toward oblivion.

Late last year I finally arranged my mother's funeral. It made sense: she was ninety-three and had substantial breast tumors, her dementia was accelerating, her abilities to feed herself and use the toilet were diminishing, she didn't always remember to chew or swallow. She was fading away. And was going to be buried back in New York, more than three thousand miles from here. Time had come—had truly come long ago—for us to plan ahead.

But my mother had always flatly refused to think about, talk about, or acknowledge the possibility of death. Bad enough she had to know there was a cemetery plot, with space reserved for her between two husbands. For my mother, preplanning a funeral would have been like walking naked in a blizzard, an open invitation to the Dark One. Never one to court bad luck, she always spat three times over her shoulder to ward off the evil eye if she accidentally mentioned being happy. No, some things were simply not to be accommodated. In his mid-nineties, when her second husband, Julius, lay comatose and dying in the hospital after a protracted illness, my mother demanded every intervention, including intubation and resuscitation, despite the wishes of her husband's family. When she learned that her brother was dying of lung cancer, she refused to visit him. Death would not be allowed near, would not be recognized.

Her sole concession had been to compel Julius to undo his own long-standing plans and agree to be buried beside her in the Skloot family plot rather than beside his first wife. Just in case, I suppose, death wasn't really Death but some endless new neighborhood, and she could guarantee husbands on either side of her throughout eternity.

In handling her financial and personal affairs over the last eight years, I tried to honor what I believed to be her wishes, even when those wishes seemed foolish, as in her maintaining an "investment portfolio" comprised entirely of a bank account and stock in one long-trusted corporation, IBM. But I came to believe that failing to preplan her funeral, like failing to maximize her remaining resources so that she could be guaranteed quality nursing home care, was not in anyone's best interests. If she'd ever been able to think about these issues rationally, she would have wanted someone to take care of matters for her properly, but just not tell her about it.

So that's what I did. I called the funeral home in New York that had handled all the Skloot burials since my family had arrived in this country. I called the funeral home on Long Island that had handled Julius' burial and read their brochure entitled "Planning for Tomorrow Today." I discussed prices and services, called two more funeral homes in New York and one in Oregon, and wondered how anyone could sort all this through when faced with grief and the urgent timing of a cross-country Jewish burial. I saw, too, the strangeness inherent in calmly prearranging a funeral, with its formalities of bereavement economics and its euphemistic glaze. You didn't have to be terrified of death to find the trappings grim. The New York funeral homes wanted me to contract with them so they could contract with an Oregon home to collect my mother, prepare her body, and ship her to New York. *Don't worry, we'll take care of Mom.* The Oregon firm wanted me to contract with them so they could contract with a New York home to collect my mother's prepared body from the airport and provide burial services. *And there's no sales tax in Oregon.* I suppose the level of planning detail and the convolutions of the funeral industry helped make this process feel sufficiently analytical and businesslike, distracting rather than lugubrious. By the end of it, I felt relief that my mother had not had to face Planning for Tomorrow Today.

Driving my mother from the doctor's office to the nursing home, we are slowed by early rush-hour traffic. She shows no signs of discomfort from her surgery, but as the road swings south and the sunlight hits her face, she swats at the glare. *Go away.* I lower the sun visors, which makes her whoop in triumph, as though the heavens had listened to her. *There!*

I'm trying to move my mind off the subject of making arrangements. But they keep insisting: bring Mother back by 4:00 for afternoon tea. Confirm that I'll be available for her Quarterly Care Conference next week, where social worker and activities coordinator and nurse and dietitian will let me know how my mother has been doing. Remember to call the cemetery in New York to discuss graveside services, the final piece of funeral business that I've been postponing because I have no idea what I want to request. Pay her bills. Plan to sell some shares of her stock in order to cover the next year's expenses.

"Where are we going?"

"To the place where you live, Mother. We'll get you there in time for tea."

"There where?"

"Not far." I've learned not to refer to it as the Nursing Home because that only confuses and upsets her, nor as Home because that makes her think we're taking her to our house, nor as Your Home because that leads us deep into Abbott and Costello Land (*I have a home? Yes! Where? Where you live. Where I live? Yes! Where?*).

"Good. But I can sing." *Three blind mice, three blind mice.*

A car swerves into our lane. I brake and tap the horn, which startles my mother and makes her arms jerk outwards and brings one into contact with my shoulder.

"Who's there?" my mother asks.

The pandemonium of my mother's mind, the highway turmoil, and the trend of my thoughts coalesce around a memory of my mother's room in New York four years ago. We were packing it up in preparation for her move to Oregon, and had found the closet and drawers in shambles. I was sitting on the floor, going through a pile of items salvaged from the jumble of old plastic bags, ancient banking records, receipts, photographs, old reminder notes, and ninety-seven packs of unopened playing cards. Without noticing what was coming along next, I lifted up a document so charged with memory that I dropped it as though shocked. Images erupted from somewhere so deep, so untapped, that I had to gasp. Beverly turned to look at me and all I could do was point.

It was a lined, cardboard accounting record, a fourteen-by-twelve manila form that I remember my father unfolding on the kitchen table in our Long Island home. January 1961, ten months before he died. I was thirteen and a half, certain to include the and-a-half whenever asked my age, and studying the stock market for my eighth-grade civics class. Suddenly, my father and I had something besides baseball to talk about. He'd just received a substantial legal settlement, three years after having been badly injured in an automobile accident. He'd set aside enough money to cover a planned summer trip to Italy, then began investing the remainder in stocks. He was new to the market, utterly engrossed by the process, and spent hours studying the newspaper's stock pages, talking about companies and what they did, what their prospects were.

For my civics course, I was required to invest an imaginary five thousand dollars in various stocks, monitor their performances over the course of a month, buy and sell, and compile careful records of what I was doing, including notes on why I made each decision. So I began to sit by my father and talk as we worked, two shrewd men of commerce sharing their opinions.

"A pretty name is a bad thing," I remember him telling me. "It's like at the track. Never bet on a horse with a fancy name."

His first major investment was thirty shares of IBM, priced then at $587.25 per share. He wrote those figures, then wrote +45 to include his broker's commission, and the total of $17,662.50 on the form's first line. Then, through his last winter and into early summer, before leaving for Italy, he filled in twenty-one more lines. They were all small investments, $827.63 for one hundred shares of Gremar Manufacturing, or $948.26 for two hundred shares of Sunset Color. He recorded his purchases in pencil, but his sales in ink. Blue or green for profits, red for the three losses, which only totaled $382.98. His biggest winner was a hundred shares of Swingline, which he sold off after eighteen days for a profit of $3,122.41.

I remember deciding to invest big, too. Follow the old man's strategy. After reading his discarded newspaper for a week, I put most of my pretend five grand into Kodak, which was marketing something new called Polaroid Land cameras. I sold my Kodak stock at the end of the term for a substantial profit and my father seemed truly proud of me. He would listen to my comments on various companies with something approaching patience, and though I remember convincing him to buy Kodak, his stock record sets me straight. He may have said he'd buy it, but I can see that he didn't.

When I held the record in my hands, when I saw his familiar but forgotten handwriting, neat and precise within the form's lines, all letters capitalized, all letters straight, I had a strong sense of his presence for the first time in decades. Then, looking on the reverse side, I saw total disarray. After my father's death in November 1961, the handwriting changes to my mother's large, swooping script, which runs wild over the lines and columns. As time goes by, and the record moves into the 1970s, the notes become unreadable, purchases and sales overlapping, stock splits drawn in with arrows, dates floating here and there, massive zones of cross-outs and ink blots, her totals in free-fall over the edges. Then there is a kind of giving-up, with her final note afloat by itself at the bottom corner: "Almost 100." By the time I took over her affairs, all that remained were descendants of those original shares of IBM that my father had bought at the beginning of 1961.

Discovering this record in her room helped me understand that disorder must always have been present in the privacy of my mother's inner world. I used to think that it was only an occasional thing, that the bedlam loosed by her moods and eruptions was a temporary aberration, a temporary chaos sundering her usual state of order. Because she did insist on order. Everything in its place and spotless, nothing to be touched or used without permission. I even had to keep my toys piled in their chest according to a sequence she determined. Disturbing her environment in any way would trigger explosive rages. External order, I believe, was her fortress against the anarchy which must have besieged her mind. Now, the thing she feared most has stormed her defenses.

I hadn't considered that angle, and try to imagine her terror as the early stages of dementia slowly took hold. Slowing onto the highway's exit, I reach over and touch my mother's shoulder. She turns to look at me.

"What's your name?"

We are in the neighborhood of the nursing home now. Exhausted, we've been singing "Three Blind Mice" in the form of a round for the past five minutes, and the words are spilling over each other as I make the last quick lefts and rights. My mother smiles, shakes her head, plunges in again after finishing her refrain.

Unable to shake the image of my father noting another sale on the record, I find myself wondering why he'd decided to enter the market when he did. He had, it seems, about thirty thousand dollars left over from the settlement. Did he have a sense that he would die within a year? Was he trying to provide a legacy for his survivors, to protect us against the mess he knew would follow his passing? That would, somehow, be a nice spin on the few facts.

The sudden influx of money seemed to free my father toward risk, something his conservative spirit had never been attracted to before. Risk for him had been driving fast, or dressing up in outlandish outfits for an annual costume party, a monthly game of pinochle. My impulse, I see, is to formulate meaning out of the fragments of memory and evidence of the record. I am trying to give it structure. But my father's motives ultimately elude me. In time, all that remained was the first safe, conservative buy: Big Blue. It's what has provided care for my mother's last lost years.

Beverly helps my mother out of the car as I unfold the walker and bring it around to her. The sun has moved behind Portland's west hills and we are all beginning to feel chilled.

"Here's your walker, Mother."

"Thank you." She grabs it, takes a couple of steps, and stops. She shakes her head.

"Is something wrong?"

"What should I do?"

"Let's go inside. It's tea time."

"But I need my walker."

"It's right here. You're already using it."

"Well of course I am. How else can I get home if you won't drive me?"

I touch her back and she begins to walk again. But it's clear that she's disturbed by something. She shakes her head again and clicks her tongue.

"It's not much further," Beverly says.

"It's too long."

"What is, Mother?"

"Everything, I guess."

It takes ten more minutes to get her into the nursing home and onto the Memory Impairment Unit. Once we are in the solarium, we help her into the seat where we'd found her earlier in the day. The dentist is asleep over his patient. Other residents are at tables, some drinking tea, and the room is filled with the familiar droning of dementia's voices that is a pattern of sound without the sense of words.

An aide, Nicole, comes over to greet my mother. "How did it go, Lillian?"

"How did what go, dear?"

"Your trip to the doctor."

My mother shakes her head. "I didn't go to the doctor." She looks around. "I never go anywhere."

I lean over to kiss her. She reaches out to touch my face, and looks at me closely. I know what she's going to say, and fight the urge to back away. Instead, I put my hand over hers and say, "It's Floyd, Mother."

CPSIA information can be obtained at www.ICGtesting.com
Printed in the USA
BVOW051500041011

272772BV00001B/39/P

9 780803 238473